MONTGOMERY COLLEGE LIBRARY
ROCKVILLE CAMPUS

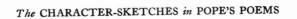

The CHARACTER-SKETCHES *in* POPE'S POEMS

POPE'S PORTRAIT OF THOMAS BETTERTON

Courtesy of the Earl of Mansfield

The CHARACTER-SKETCHES *in* POPE'S POEMS

by

BENJAMIN BOYCE

Durham, N. C.
DUKE UNIVERSITY PRESS
1 9 6 2

PR
3634
R7106303 B65
1962

© 1962, DUKE UNIVERSITY PRESS

Library of Congress Catalog Card number 62-10050

Cambridge University Press, London N.W. 1, England

Printed in the United States of America
by the Seeman Printery, Inc., Durham, N. C.

PREFATORY NOTE

In quoting the text of Pope's sketches I have used when possible the first published editions. Only thus could his revisions be conveniently discussed. Line-numbers, therefore, ordinarily refer to the text of the first edition. In quotations I have followed modern usage in italics and in the *i-j, u-v* spellings. Unless otherwise noted, the place of publication of works cited is London.

Quotation from the Twickenham Edition of the *Poems of Alexander Pope* is made by permission of the Yale University Press and Methuen and Company, publishers respectively in this country and in England. Quotation from George Sherburn's edition of Pope's *Correspondence* is made by permission of the Clarendon Press.

Special thanks are due to Professor Sherburn for many useful suggestions and to the Earl of Mansfield for kind permission to reproduce as frontispiece Pope's portrait of Thomas Betterton. The Council on Research of Duke University has greatly assisted me with grants in aid of travel and publication.

B. B.

Contents

Abbreviations *and* Short Titles

Ault and Butt = *Alexander Pope Minor Poems,* ed. Norman Ault and John Butt (Twickenham Edition, Vol. VI). 1954

Bateson = *Alexander Pope Epistles to Several Persons (Moral Essays),* ed. F. W. Bateson (Twickenham Edition, Vol. III, ii). 1951

Butt = *Alexander Pope Imitations of Horace,* ed. John Butt (Twickenham Edition, Vol. IV). 2d ed., 1953

Caractères = *Les Caracteres de Theophraste . . . avec Les Caracteres ou les Moeurs de ce Siecle, Par M. de la Bruyere.* 3 vols. Amsterdam, 1720

Correspondence = *The Correspondence of Alexander Pope,* ed. George Sherburn. 5 vols. Oxford, 1956

Elwin-Courthope = *The Works of Alexander Pope,* ed. W. Elwin and W. J. Courthope. 10 vols. 1871-89

Mack = *Alexander Pope An Essay on Man,* ed. Maynard Mack (Twickenham Edition, Vol. III, i). 1950

Spence = Joseph Spence, *Anecdotes, Observations, and Characters,* ed. Samuel W. Singer. 1820

Sutherland = *Alexander Pope The Dunciad,* ed. Jas. Sutherland (Twickenham Edition, Vol. V). 2d ed., 1953

Epistle to a Lady = *Of the Characters of Women: An Epistle to a Lady. By Mr. Pope . . . MDCCXXXV*

Epistle to Lord Bathurst = *Of the Use of Riches, An Epistle To the Right Honorable Allen Lord Bathurst. By Mr. Pope . . . 1732*

Epistle to Dr. Arbuthnot = *An Epistle from Mr. Pope, to Dr. Arbuthnot . . . 1734*

Epistle to Lord Burlington = *An Epistle to the Right Honourable Richard Earl of Burlington. Occasion'd by his Publishing Palladio's Designs . . . By Mr. Pope . . . MDCCXXXI*

Epistle to Lord Cobham = *An Epistle to the Right Honourable Richard Lord Visc^t. Cobham. By Mr. Pope . . . 1733*

The CHARACTER-SKETCHES *in* POPE'S POEMS

CHAPTER I

INTRODUCTION

POPE'S earliest surviving poem is a character-sketch. And the
"morality" which he like Socrates distributed from his deathbed[1]
depended for its force upon numerous character-sketches. Between
1700, when according to Pope he had written the "Ode on Solitude,"
and 1744, when his *Epistles* were at last prepared for publication in
the form that included the awe-inspiring figures of Cloe, Atossa, and
Philomede, Pope composed at least sixty sketches ranging in length
from four lines to the seventy-line picture of Aristarchus in the
Dunciad Book IV. There were also countless fragmentary characterizations struck off in a line or two, but these are not fully designed
pictures, and I shall not consider them here. Although Pope once
said he disliked attacking particular persons, he was very responsive
to the people about him, and more frequently than Horace or Boileau
he enlivened his poems with well-defined pictures of types and
individuals.

To be sure, in the beautifully finished lines of *The Rape of the
Lock* there are no full, composed character-sketches beyond the not
quite reliable words about Belinda's sprightly mind and sweetness.
In the original *Dunciad*, the most famous of Augustan personal
satires, there is very little of interest of this sort—only the fanciful
dramatizing of the hero in Book I, glimpses of the clumsy figures of
Lintot, Tonson, and Moore-Smythe in Book II, and the brief carica-
tures of Herne and Henley in Book III. But in the *Miscellanies* and

---

1. " 'Here am I, like Socrates, distributing my morality among my friends, just
as I am dying.'—P. [This was said on his sending about some of his Ethic Epistles,
as presents, about three weeks before we lost him."—Spence, p. 318.

fugitive verse, in the *Epistles* and "imitations" of Horace and Donne, in the early poems and the late *Dunciad* Book IV one finds an abundance of carefully executed pictures of men and women, various in tone and manner but almost always effective. A few years ago Norman Ault wrote an essay to celebrate Pope the landscape-painter and scene-painter in verse, Pope the user of colors in poetry.[2] Yet in the surviving lists, serious and comical, of the actual canvases which he produced in the studio of his friend Charles Jervas during the year and a half he was working there, no landscapes are mentioned. For Jervas and his pupil were painting people. "I have thrown away," Pope cheerfully informed John Caryll in a letter of August 31, 1713, "three Dr Swifts, two Dutchesses of Montague, one Virgin Mary, the Queen of England, besides half a score earls and a Knight of the Garter."[3] Of the portraits he did not throw away only one or two are now known to exist.[4] But three-score portraits in verse are preserved to us.

It must be acknowledged at the outset that there are hazards and pitfalls in the path of him who would offer comment on this aspect of Pope's work. It has been usually assumed, to mention a question which will be considered more carefully later, that Dryden was Pope's master in the art of character-drawing. There is truth in that assumption, of course, but it scants too much. Dryden's contemporaries in satire, especially John Sheffield (first Duke of Buckinghamshire and Normanby), were probably almost as important influences on his method as Dryden was on his versification. Elijah Fenton wrote to William Broome in 1729, during the storm aroused by the *Dunciad Variorum*, that Pope had recently declared that "for the future he intended to write nothing but epistles in Horace's manner,"[5] and certainly Pope learned a good deal about satiric portraiture from Horace. But I suspect he learned as much from Juvenal, and if Edward Young in the preface of his *Love of Fame* (1728) had not

---

2. See the chapter, "Mr Alexander Pope: Painter," in his *New Light on Pope* (1949).

3. *Correspondence*, I, 189.

4. See Appendix A.

5. *Correspondence*, III, 37.

announced the superiority of Horace's delicacy and laughter to Juvenal's harshness, perhaps Pope might somewhere have acknowledged Juvenal as one of his masters. As for Theophrastus, the ancient originator of the fine art of the literary "Character," one might expect his distinctive and admirable technique to have contributed to that of Pope. But though Pope knew Theophrastus, as most educated people did, and though one of his satiric *jeux d'esprit* was inspired by Theophrastus,[6] he shows more indebtedness to the broad tradition of Character-writing in later times than to the ancient writer himself. The models for Pope's art were numerous.

More familiar are the problems arising out of the tantalizing uncertainty that hangs about the identity of many of the figures in Pope's poems. The temptation to find living originals and to fall victim to what is nowadays called the intentional heresy is more than many readers have been able to withstand. To what degree the likelihood of error is increased by Pope's habit of revising and rearranging his verses no one can appreciate until he has tried to master all the details of these changes. The fact is that Pope in developing his sketches seems to have been as attentive to books and literary effect as to people. We may therefore understand his work, including his use of personalities, a little better if we consider also the relationship between various of his sketches and their possible literary originals and models. Apropos of such connections I should say that I hope the reader will not be immediately horrified into rebellion by the suggestion that Pope possibly derived a hint or two from the "dunce" William Law, from the patron saint of dunces Richard Flecknoe, and from Mrs. Mary Delariviere Manley, who according to Sir Winston Churchill "cannot be swept incontinently back into the cesspool from which she should never have crawled."[7] Flecknoe's prose Characters are not the part of his work that established his picturesque notoriety; and no matter how sordid the charms of Mrs. Manley's books, she was read by everybody, and the student of Pope's day ought not to ignore her.

6. See below pp. 60-61.
7. *Marlborough His Life and Times,* I (1933), 130.

The skill with which Pope made tone and imagery and diction support his meaning has recently been analyzed in several admirable studies; his repertoire of irony and persuasion is now becoming familiar. But attention to the "total" design, to poetic texture, and to the personae of the major poems has somehow mostly left out of consideration the schemes and traditions of his character-sketches. One aspect of his work which, if not always strictly poetic, is none the less literary remains to be studied—the degree and kind of success he achieved as a painter of people. To this latter question the present study is directed with the hope of enriching our sense of Pope's accomplishment. Some familiarity with the periodical essays and the humorous novels of the eighteenth century as well as a glance into the eighteenth-century British rooms in any good art museum should prepare one for Johnson's complaint in *Idler* Number 45 that "the painters find no encouragement among the English for many other works than portraits." Pope lived in a society addicted to portraiture,[8] and this aspect of his writing, though only one element in his aesthetic vision, merits some attention.

It may be thought, however, that an apology is in order for my venturing to treat the sketches so frequently out of context. But since many of the descriptions, including those of Sylvia, Artimesia, Atticus, Cloe, the backbiter, and perhaps Atossa, were separate verse-compositions originally, and since the large portrait of Marlborough was apparently written for a context it did not fit, there should be some propriety in considering these and other pieces for what they are in themselves. From Horace to Pope the tradition of verse-satire included as one of its weapons and embellishments the depiction of real and imaginary persons. But Pope's pictures surpass those of Horace and Boileau in concentration and brilliance and those of Dryden in abundance and range. My concern is with the art and the craft of Pope's character-sketching.

---

8. Hanging on the walls of Pope's villa in Twickenham, presumably at the time of his death, were at least sixty portraits. Probably many of the other seventy-odd prints and paintings of unspecified subjects were also portraits. See *Notes and Queries,* 6th ser., V, 363-365.

In his poems Pope did not ordinarily desire simplicity. To seek for simple generalizations about the purposes and tendencies in his work might turn out to be worse than useless. His poetry is richer, more reflective of human nature pleasant and unpleasant, more delightful to the intellect, more beautiful to the sensibilities, and certainly more various, than would allow for plain and dogmatic conclusions. I feel no embarrassment, therefore, in saying that the material I shall present sometimes seems to point in opposite directions. Pope's poetry was composed by a man who did not always produce the same kind or the same quality of work, and for the student of poetic art his works are interesting in part because in the surviving manuscripts and numerous published revisions one can often see how the mind and fingers of a gifted and devoted writer worked under the pressure of different sorts of impulses.

CHAPTER II

The CHOICE *of* SUBJECTS

TYPES *and* INDIVIDUALS

A hundred smart in Timon and in Balaam:
The fewer still you name, you wound the more;
B-nd is but one, but Harpax is a Score.

(*The First Satire of the Second
Book of Horace, Imitated*, 1733)

LITERARY character-sketches may be divided into two kinds. One kind portrays an individual. It represents the essential features of the man with enough attention to special idiosyncrasies to make his identity separate from that of other men. Of course all intellectual activity is carried on by comparison and definition; we learn to know Mr. A by noticing that in some respects he is like Mr. B or is not like Mr. B, and so on through a suitable list of possibilities. Hence a portrait of one person inevitably suggests some resemblances—in cast of mind or shape of body, in a trick of gesture or failure in morals—between its subject and certain other people. Yet the *tout ensemble* of features is unique and as such interesting, and it is in order to reveal this that the portrait of an individual ordinarily exists.

The opposite kind of character-sketch presents a type. It attempts to evoke an image of a whole class of men in a hypothetical figure who interests us not for himself chiefly but because in some significant feature or features he is like everybody else in that class. "True, true, true," the reader mutters as more and more specimens are spitted by the writer's pen. The idiosyncrasies of any one member of the class are for the time being ignored as negligible modifications of the central form. We are not now attempting to be fair to every human soul. Identity with a special group of people is what this kind of picture exists to portray.

Though the dichotomy between portraits of individuals and pictures of types is a real one, the distinction sometimes seems a relative matter. For example, if a conscientious writer of history goes to the trouble of drawing a portrait, he ordinarily strives for a fair resemblance even if the occasion does not require that he pursue every aspect of character until he achieves a complete revelation. The aim in such work is a plausible organization of mostly verifiable fact. But on another occasion the historian like the satirist may deliberately ignore many facts and narrow the portrait to symbolize an idea or suggest a social current. The individual has lost part of his individuality and has become a type, a semi-theoretical figure. "B-nd is but one, but Harpax is a Score," wrote Pope; yet Denis Bond, though a particular swindler, serves chiefly, at least at our distance, to suggest a whole crowd of greedy, shameless men in high place.

One distinction, obvious enough in theory, has often been forgotten by annotators of Pope: a portrait may be drawn of an actual individual, or it may be composed about an imaginary individual. (We need not worry at this point over the likelihood that everybody's view of everybody else should be recognized as imaginary. Nor need we delay over the question of the inescapable modification of historical reality that in some degree occurs in even the most faithful portraiture.) Regardless of the traditions of neo-classical poetry, it is possible that a poet may draw out of his own invention a figure as unusual and complex as any to be found in the pages of Clarendon or Burnet.

What I have been saying would not have been news to Alexander Pope. In his later years, if not before, he could have had no doubt that the genuinely intended depiction of a type may remind a reader of someone in particular, or conversely, that the most delicately accurate portrait of a unique being may suggest something pervasive in a certain portion of human society. Out of these glints and ambiguities must have come half the fun he had in writing his *Epistles* and his *Horace*.

Out of these delicious glints and partly intentional ambiguities have come also the labors of numerous students of Pope. At the beginning were William Warburton and Joseph Warton and Horace Walpole, each of whom drew red herrings across our path, though only Warburton seems to have done so deliberately. Walpole's satisfaction in naming "originals" for Pope's ridiculous and contemptible pictures belonged to his own temperament and was without the responsibilities and temptations that sometimes twisted the remarks of Warburton, Pope's strong-willed official editor. A safer guide than any of these would be Edward Harley, the second Earl of Oxford, Pope's generous friend, who when identifying even so plain a case as Sporus in the *Epistle to Dr. Arbuthnot* cautiously avoided dogmatism: "It so happens [he noted in his own copy of the poem] that this is generaly applyed to Lord Hervey, and as he deserved it of Mr Pope, it is very proper for him & is very justly Drawn."[1] From the beginning, readers of Pope have continued to see the possibilities of personal allusions in his sketches and have tried to resolve the mysteries with quite remarkable assurance. Which of Pope's sketches, they ask, were intended to portray whole classes of men and which to reveal someone in particular? Much more exciting, who was the someone in particular?

The fact that on occasion Pope did not describe a character but only specified him in a line or phrase seems not to have discouraged efforts at identification in Pope's day or later. Witness Lady Mary Wortley Montagu's seeing herself in the appalling couplet,

> From furious Sappho yet a sadder Fate,
> P—x'd by her Love, or libell'd by her Hate.
>
> (*Horace*, Sat., II, i)[2]

Witness, too, the determination of annotators to find the originals of such incompletely outlined figures as Delia ("Slander or Poyson, dread from Delia's Rage"—*Horace*, Sat., II, i) or Catius—

---

1. Bodleian Library, shelf-mark M. 3. 19 Art.
2. See Butt, p. xvii.

> Catius is ever moral, ever grave,
> Thinks who endures a knave, is next a knave;
> Save just at Dinner—then prefers, no doubt,
> A Rogue with Ven'son to a Saint without.[3]

Patritio in the *Epistle to Lord Cobham* is Sidney Godolphin, said Warburton, and most editors adopt this identification as if certainly right while rejecting as if certainly wrong Warburton's saying that the woman complimented at the end of the *Epistle to a Lady* is not Martha Blount or any other of Pope's acquaintance. Calypso in the latter poem represents Anne Griffith and Narcissa is Elizabeth Gerard, said Walpole, ignoring the implications of the circumstance that both the sketches are fragments of an earlier account of someone called Sylvia. The "rev'rend sire," father of a nameless race, mentioned in the *Epistle to Lord Cobham* was said by Walpole to be Lancelot Blackburne, Archbishop of York; but Lord Cobham, writing to Pope about this passage before it was printed, spoke only of "the old Letcher" and thought "the instance it self is but ordinary."[4] Cloe in the *Epistle to a Lady*, according to Warton, Walpole, and Malone, represents Mrs. Howard, Lady Suffolk; yet there are plain indications that neither she nor Pope supposed that people would see much resemblance to her in Cloe.[5]

A survey of these and other mistaken certainties and insufficiently grounded guesses should encourage the industrious annotator to exercise more often his negative capabilities. Yet Pope's own uncertainties and reticences sometimes are enough to lead one into temptation and then into bewilderment. In an early draft of the *Epistle to Lord Bathurst* Pope mentioned one rich miser named "S—k" whom he called Harpax in the printed text and another rich, wretched miser named Worldly whom in the printed text he called Shylock. In the

---

3. *Epistle to Lord Cobham*, p. 8. For Carruther's unlikely suggestion that Catius represented Charles Dartineuf, see Bateson, p. 24 n.

4. *Correspondence*, III, 391-392. Cobham in a second letter about this poem (III, 393) says that in place of the lecher and "Glutton" (Helluo), who are simply indulging a natural impulse, "a Cardinal in his way of pleasure would have been a better instance."

5. Norman Ault, *New Light on Pope* (1949), pp. 266-275.

first printed text of the poem he mentioned the avaricious speculator "S-l——k" but in subsequent editions called this person Shylock, thus making two characters of that name within the poem. In the *Epistle to Lord Cobham* there is a miser Shylock, but in a leaf of the printed text preserved by Warburton Pope had crossed out that name and written in "Selkirk" instead.[6] In the first edition (1737) of Pope's imitation of Horace's second Epistle in Book Two a penurious man is called "D***," perhaps for the Duke of Devonshire; but in the text of this poem in one of the octavo editions of Pope's *Works* (1738) the fellow is called "Van-muck," perhaps for J. Vanneck, a would-be purchaser of Bolingbroke's Dawley Farm.[7] In his imitation of Horace's first Satire in Book Two Pope uses the line which I have already quoted about Delia, a fearful lady whose rage drives her into offering slander or poison. But in the Chauncy manuscript[8] the line reads: "Slander or lies expect from W—y's rage"—perhaps because Pope was thinking about Lady Mary Wortley Montagu. Is one to assume that no vestige of "W—y" remains in "Delia," whom some annotators feel sure was the Countess of Delorain?[9]

Pope laughed at the dauber "who not being able to draw Portraits after the Life, was used to paint Faces at Random, and look out afterwards for People whom he might persuade to be like them."[10] His friend Edward Harley recorded a similar thought: "It is with writers of characters as with Taylors who make suits of all sorts and for all seises without taking measure of particular persons, people come afterwards of their own accord and fit themselves to them."[11] But something like this is bound to happen even in the best writers, and Pope's mirth need not be taken very seriously, least of all when one notices such revisions as have just been mentioned. In fact he more

---

6. See Bateson, *passim*, for these facts.

7. Butt, p. 181 n.

8. Elwin-Courthope, III, 295.

9. Butt, p. 12 n.

10. *Guardian* No. 4 (*The Prose Works of Alexander Pope*, ed. Norman Ault [Oxford, 1936], I, 77). An earlier expression of the idea can be found in a letter from Pope to Lord Lansdowne in 1713 (*Correspondence*, I, 172).

11. British Museum MS Loan 29/349.

than once alluded to the curious way nature has of justifying the imagination:

> Feign what I will, and paint it e'er so strong,
> Some rising Genius sins up to my Song.
>
> (*One Thousand Seven Hundred and Thirty Eight,*
Dialogue II, ll. 8-9)

Art, including the satirist's art, works its spell by re-organization and by suggestion. As for the artist himself, the likelihood is that by 1743-44 Pope himself could not have said to what degree many of his sketches were particular or general or where exactly each of the figures had originated. And modern judgment concerning the typicality or individuality of many of the sketches will inevitably be subjective and variable.

What the accepted literary theory was in the Augustan period is plain enough. One would not deny Horace, who talks us into sense. When portraying figures in poetry, "Either follow tradition or invent what is self-consistent. If haply, when you write, you bring back to the stage the honouring of Achilles, let him be impatient, passionate, ruthless, fierce; let him claim that laws are not for him, let him ever make appeal to the sword. Let Medea be fierce and unyielding, Ino tearful, Ixion forsworn, Io a wanderer, Orestes sorrowful. If it is an untried theme you entrust to the stage, and if you boldly fashion a fresh character, have it kept to the end even as it came forth at the first, and have it self-consistent."[12]

But if one looks into Horace's first Epistle, a poem that Pope modernized, one may be disconcerted to find him declaring that men are capricious and changeable and, one gathers, hardly susceptible to consistent representation:

> But show me one, who has it in his pow'r
> To act consistent with himself an hour.

Nevertheless the ancient doctrine that men fall into permanent classes and that the orator and the poet should recognize the types had be-

---

12. *De Arte Poetica*, ll. 119-127 (*Horace Satires, Epistles . . . with an English Translation by H. Rushton Fairclough*, Loeb Classical Library [1955], p. 461).

come obligatory a century before Pope's day. The theory of the ruling passion was one way of seeming to subscribe to the law.

Good manners, another shibboleth in both literature and society in the Augustan world, also demanded that one avoid personalities even in satire. The *Spectator* in Number 34 promised "never to draw a faulty Character which does not fit at least a Thousand People." In Number 262 Addison declared: "[W]hen I draw any faulty Character, I consider all those Persons to whom the Malice of the World may possibly apply it, and take care to dash it with such particular Circumstances as may prevent all such ill-natured Applications." Not to discourage ill nature so much as to solicit contributions, the *Spectator* in Number 442 offered an amusing list of the classes that make up society and from which he would welcome literary contributions:

all manner of Persons, whether Scholars, Citizens, Courtiers, Gentlemen of the Town or Country, and all Beaux, Rakes, Smarts, Prudes, Coquets, Housewives, and all Sorts of Wits, whether Male or Female, and however distinguish'd, whether . . . Arch, Dry, Natural, Acquir'd, Genuine, or Deprav'd Wits; and Persons of all Sorts of Tempers and Complexions, whether the Severe, the Delightful, the Impertinent, . . . the Serene or Cloudy, Jovial or Melancholy . . . and of what Manners or Dispositions soever, whether the Ambitious or Humble-minded, the Proud or Pitiful . . . and under what Fortune or Circumstance soever, whether the Contented or Miserable, . . . Rich or Poor (whether so thro' Want of Money, or Desire of more) . . . Marry'd or Single . . . Fat or Lean; and of what Trade, Occupation, . . . Faction, Party, . . . Age or Condition soever . . . .

The unabbreviated list might convince anyone that personalities are quite unnecessary in a writer's repertoire.

Every reader of Pope's poems can point to numerous plainly typical figures among the sketches. One may begin with the wistfully drawn retired man in the "Ode on Solitude," the incorruptible literary critic and the bookful-blockhead critic in the third part of the *Essay on Criticism*, Timon (certainly a type, whatever Pope's enemies might say) and all the other figures in the *Epistle to Lord Burlington.* In the *Epistle to Lord Bathurst* one finds the careful sketches of the miser, old Cotta, and of the extravagant man, Cotta's son. Near the end of the *Epistle to Lord Cobham* are a string of briefly but brightly drawn type-figures, including the lecherous old man, the glutton Helluo, the miserly old woman, the vain Narcissa, and the money-lover Euclio. In the *Epistle to a Lady* are Rufa, Sappho, and Papillia the changeable lady. In the fourth book of the *Dunciad* the flower-fancier, the butterfly-collector, the dissipated young man returning from the Grand Tour, and the materialistic philosopher are conspicuous type-sketches. Some of Pope's epitaphs and, in *Miscellanies. The Last Volume* (1727), three sketches—the mannish bluestocking Artimesia, the successful whore Phryne, and perhaps the literary toady Umbra—should be added to the list. In this assemblage of about thirty sketches we see that Pope had made a sufficient oblation before the shrine of consistency and typicality in characterization.

But difficulties arise as one compiles such a list. Should Umbra be listed as a type of literary parasite, or is he really a once-recognizable caricature of Eustace Budgell?[13] Should Bufo in the *Epistle to Dr. Arbuthnot* be entered as a type of the self-indulgent patron of the arts, or is he to give pleasure to the reader as one of the many contemporary scornful pictures of the Earl of Halifax, in this case remade from lines describing George Bubb Dodington? And is the bard mentioned in that poem for his pilfered pastorals (Butt, l. 179) a type of the hack-writer, or is he recognizably Ambrose Philips? Was Cloe, a heartless lady, meant especially to rebuke a cruel Miss Foley?[14] Should Aristarchus in *Dunciad* Book IV be mentioned here as chiefly a type of the pedant and misguided philologian of Pope's day even if he is recognizable also as Richard Bentley? Do the Man of Ross and George Villiers in the *Epistle to Lord Bathurst* seem more than just types of the Christian philanthropist and the selfish rake? In both depictions, one learns, there are falsifications of fact, introduced no doubt in order that each man's life might illustrate Pope's generalizations.

---

13. See Ault and Butt, pp. 140-141.
14. Ault, *New Light on Pope*, pp. 266-275.

Among the deliberate, recognizable portraits in the poems are the complimentary drawings of Horace and Walsh in the *Essay on Criticism,* of Sir William Trumbull in *Windsor Forest,* of Bolingbroke (*Essay on Man,* IV, 373-382 [Mack]), of Craggs (in the Epistle addressed to him), of Mrs. Howard (in "On a certain Lady at Court"), of John Kyrle the " Man of Ross," and of Pope's father (in the *Epistle to Dr. Arbuthnot*).[15] The satiric portraits of Addison ("Atticus"), Ambrose Philips ("Macer"),[16] Lord Hervey ("Sporus"), Richard Bentley ("Aristarchus"), the Duke of Wharton ("Clodio"), George Villiers Duke of Buckingham, Peter Walter (in *The Second Satire of Dr. John Donne . . . Versifyed*), Moore-Smythe (*Dunciad,* II, 33-46), Sir John Blunt (*Epistle to Lord Bathurst*), the Duke of Marlborough,[17] and Halifax ("Bufo") can all be identified, with the exception of the last, fairly certainly. By drawing on the two-score epitaphs that Pope wrote, one can add to the list of truly revealing, personal portraits only two, those of John Gay and the Earl of Dorset. Of the rest, many of which are little more than epigrams, the lines on Caryll, Trumbull, Craggs, Fenton, Digby, Withers, Knight, and Mrs. Corbet evoke, as most epitaphs do, images of types. The fact that Pope could transfer the first six lines of the epitaph on Lord Caryll, a Catholic Jacobite, to his epitaph on Sir William Trumbull, a staunch servant of King William, indicates the nature of most of these pieces. In trying to state essentials briefly the poet must neglect characteristic distinctions.

Another interesting group of sketches consists of portraits of individualized figures that were, so far as one can now learn, either altogether imaginary or deliberately altered copies of real people.

15. Perhaps Pope's lines about himself in his imitations of Horace (Epistles, I, i; Satires II, i and ii) and in the *Epistle to Dr. Arbuthnot* should be added to the list of complimentary portraits even though Elder Olson ("Rhetoric and the Appreciation of Pope," *Modern Philol.,* XXXVII [1939], 13-35) and Maynard Mack ("The Muse of Satire," *Yale Review,* XLI [1951-52], 80-92) would have us see some of these passages as adaptations of the traditional image of the classical orator, persuasive because seemingly virtuous.

16. First printed in *Miscellanies. The Last Volume* (1727); Ault and Butt, pp. 137-139.

17. See below pp. 69-70.

Any list of these pieces will vary according to one's opinions on numerous debatable cases. I should put here the drawings of Sylvia[18] (one of Pope's most striking creations), Fufidia,[19] the foppish disloyal friend of the poet (*Epistle to Dr. Arbuthnot*, ll. 291-304 [Butt]), Sir Balaam (*Epistle to Lord Bathurst*), Patritio and the gay freethinker (*Epistle to Lord Cobham*), and, in the *Epistle to a Lady*, Silia, Narcissa, Calypso, Flavia, Atossa, Cloe, and Philomede.

In Pope's poems altogether the sketches that are interesting because they especially evoke a whole class of people are balanced arithmetically if not indeed also aesthetically by those that pique the reader with glimpses of special, unique personalities. Such a balance is fortunate. Tastes vary. Some of us relish types; others, less addicted to generalization, prefer novelty. Pope liked to draw both kinds of figures, but in his theoretical utterances he gave his authority to the individual character, for there his intuitions (as well as, on occasion, certain writers) led him.

Perhaps it was intuition, perhaps it was Addison, that caused Pope to say of Shakespeare in 1725 that every single character of his "is as much an Individual, as those in Life itself; it is as impossible to find any two alike; and such as from their relation or affinity in any respect appear most to be Twins, will upon comparison be found remarkably distinct."[20] The same sort of admiration for absolute "Distinction of Characters" had been implied in a footnote in Pope's

---

18. First printed in *Miscellanies. The Last Volume* (1727); Ault and Butt, pp. 286-288.

19. *Sober Advice from Horace* (*Sat.*, I, ii), ll. 17-25.

20. Preface, *The Works of Shakespear* (1725), I, iii. Cf. *Spectator* Number 273: "Homer has excelled all the heroic Poets that ever wrote, in the multitude and variety of his Characters. . . . His Princes are as much distinguished by their Manners as by their Dominions; and even those among them, whose Characters seem wholly made up of Courage, differ from one another as to the particular kinds of Courage in which they excell. In short, there is scarce a Speech or Action in the *Iliad*, which the Reader may not ascribe to the Person that speaks or acts, without seeing his Name at the Head of it."

It was this assertion of Pope's which was undoubtedly in Dr. Johnson's mind when he said in the preface to his edition of Shakespeare (in which edition Pope's preface was to be reprinted) that in "the writings of other poets a character is too often an individual; in those of Shakespeare it is commonly a species."

Iliad. Andromache's lament (*Iliad*, XXII, 606-661) could "be spoken properly by none but Andromache: There is nothing general in her Sorrows, nothing that can be transfer'd to another Character." Such commentary, with its unblushing indifference to the opposite theory of typical, representative characterization, prepares one better than Horace for Pope's subsequent defenses of personal satire and for his poetic practice, early and late.

After the unexpected reception of his *Epistle to Lord Burlington* and the charge that the poem ridiculed the Duke of Chandos, Pope wrote to John Caryll that in his next poem he would "make living examples, which inforce best" when one wishes to advance moral and religious virtue.[21] In the *Epistle to Lord Bathurst* (1732) he did as he had promised, quite outstripping Horace in the bold mention of egregious contemporaries. Within the first two hundred lines a curious reader could put his wits to work to identify "W-rd," "W-t-rs," "Ch—rs," "H-wl-y," "Tu**r," "Wh**n," "H*p*s," "B*nd," "Sir G**t," "Bl*t," "Rev'rend S**n," and "S-l-k." All of these gutted names were filled in for the 1735 edition except two which were supplanted by other names then or later. All of the men alluded to were alive when the poem was first printed except Blunt, Turner, Wharton, and Chartres, and those four had died very recently.

More than a year later, in August, 1734, Dr. Arbuthnot sent to Pope as his "Last Request" an exhortation to continue to assail vice, but to do it more discreetly, with the purpose of reforming, not chastising. Pope replied:

I would indeed do it with more restrictions, & less personally; it is more agreeable to my nature, which those who know it not are greatly mistaken in: But General Satire in Times of General Vice has no force, & is no Punishment: People have ceas'd to be ashamed of it when so many are joind with them; and tis only by hunting One or two from the Herd that any Examples can be made. If a man writ all his Life against the Collective Body of the Banditti, or against Lawyers, would it do the least Good, or lessen the Body? But if some are hung up, or pilloryed, it may prevent others. And in my low Station . . . I hope to deter, if not to reform.[22]

---

21. *Correspondence*, III, 316.
22. *Correspondence*, III, 423.

Pope's expanded and revised version of the same letter justifies the use of particular examples rather than precepts: "Examples are pictures, and strike the Senses, nay raise the Passions, and call in those (the strongest and most general of all motives) to the aid of reformation . . . . The only sign by which I found my writings ever did any good, or had any weight, has been that they rais'd the anger of bad men."[23]

Some four years after that exchange of letters Pope published his *One Thousand Seven Hundred and Thirty Eight. Dialogue II* as a defense against friends and enemies who like the dying Arbuthnot and like Edward Young in his *Two Epistles to Mr. Pope* (1730) wished him to "strike faults, but spare the man." Pope justifies himself tartly and with good reason. Richard Steele in an unexpected mood of penitential reform once exhorted fellow-soldiers when fighting to "Pursue without Cruelty, and Stab without Hatred."[24] But success in neither war nor satire, I imagine, comes that sweetly if the enemy is really threatening. (Anyone who has published satire or fought in hand-to-hand battle may correct me if I am wrong.) In his later satires Pope assailed some of the most serious and dangerous flaws in the social structure, and he did so in no namby-pamby way. Like Samuel Johnson he was a man of great physical courage. His satire was at times deliberately personal, and when the cause was just he needed—indeed today needs—no apology. Though with us two centuries later the symbolic aspects of his sketches may necessarily be more effective, the particular allusions must have been strong and startling and very sobering at the time the poems were published. It would be an injustice to Pope to minimize or deplore his achieved capacity to alarm guilty individuals.

To be sure, in certain publications he seemed to deny to his readers the interest and satisfaction of personal allusion. The first edition of the *Epistle to a Lady* was prefaced by the anonymous author's "Advertisement" as follows:

---

23. *Correspondence*, III, 419.
24. *The Christian Hero*, ed. Rae Blanchard (Oxford, 1932), p. 10.

The Author being very sensible how particular a Tenderness is due to the FEMALE SEX, and at the same time how little they generally show to each other; declares, upon his Honour, that no one Character is drawn from the Life, in this Epistle. It would otherwise be most improperly ascribed to a Lady, who, of all the Women he knows, is the last that would be entertain'd at the Expence of Another.

There is a curious resemblance between the ambiguous gallantry to the fair sex and compliment to the dedicatee in these words and a similar combination of gallantry and compliment near the beginning of Edward Young's first satire on women, published eight years before:

> The Sex we honour, tho' their faults we blame;
> May thank their faults for such a fruitful Theme.
> A theme, fair ——! doubly kind to me,
> Since satyrizing those, is praising thee;
> Who wouldst not bear, too modestly refin'd,
> A panegyrick of a grosser kind.[25]

Pope was, one sees, improving upon the justification offered by Young for presenting a set of satiric sketches of women at the same time he obeyed Young's injunction to "strike faults, but spare the man."

But about four months later when Pope included the *Epistle to a Lady* in the octavo edition of his *Works* he added a footnote that casts a different light over the earlier "Advertisement" and also over the author's intentions in that poem. The footnote apologizes for a "Want of Connection" at certain points

occasioned by the omission of certain Examples and Illustrations to the Maxims laid down, which may put the Reader in mind of what the Author has said in his Imitation of Horace,
> Publish the present Age, but where the Text
> Is Vice too high, reserve it for the next.

To infer that the omitted sketches came close to particular persons would not seem unjustified. Pope was carrying on the game already

---

25. *The Universal Passion. Satire* V (1727), pp. 1-2.

played by the "dunces" Welsted and Moore-Smythe in *One Epistle to Mr. A. Pope* (1730), in which several times in place of a line of verse they offer a line of asterisks, footnoting one such line thus: "The Characters left out here may perhaps be inserted in some future Editions of this Poem."

Pope had another game to play once in a while. This is the trick of fixing an identification by soberly discussing and denying it. In two 1735 editions of the *Dunciad* the couplet—

> Whence hapless Monsieur much complains at Paris
> Of wrongs from Duchesses and Lady Mary's—

is given a footnote informing the reader that this passage "was thought to allude to a famous Lady who cheated a French wit of 5000 pounds in the South-Sea year. But the Author meant it in general of all bragging Travellers, and of all Whores and Cheats under the name of Ladies."[26] Any "insiders" who had missed the allusion to Lady Mary and M. Rémond would now have it. Outsiders would at least see that other matters might be thought of than the comical habit of Drury Lane whores of assuming the names of great ladies and famous beauties.[27] Better still in this game was the gratuitous footnote in the *Dunciad* (III, 184) protesting that it was wrong to suppose that the dull sober antiquary Wormius is "our own Antiquary Mr. Thomas Herne."

That Pope was at least piqued by personal satire is obvious. Anyone who has harbored the pleasant illusion that he was not should examine Pope's own copy of *A New Collection of Poems Relating to State Affairs, from Oliver Cromwel To this present Time: By the Greatest Wits of the Age* (1705).[28] The contents of the volume are almost entirely pieces of a personal sort—lampoons, epigrams, "Instructions to a Painter" (ten such poems), blunt and coarse satires

---

26. Sutherland, p. 112 n.

27. See Aubrey L. Williams, "Pope's 'Duchesses and Lady Mary's,'" *Review of English Studies*, N.S. IV (1953), 359-361.

28. British Museum shelf-number C.28.e.15. See my discussion of this volume in *Notes and Queries*, N.S. V (1958), 55-57, and pp. 291-294, 437-438, for further commentary by W. J. Cameron and Geoffrey Tillotson.

on kings, princes, statesmen, ladies, generals, poets, and what not. Pope seems to have gone through the volume from the beginning to the end, reading satire after satire acrid with abuse and nastiness and using his pen to fill in the gutted names and blanks or identifying people in marginal notes altogether about four hundred times in the 591 pages. King Charles and King James, Buckingham and Halifax, Dorset and Dryden and Addison, Villiers and Marborough, bishops and lecherous peeresses—Pope was impelled by what seems either genuine interest or an editorial passion to specify them all. He was even busier with annotations at the end of the volume than earlier. One thinks of the request made by his friend Swift for full notes for the *Dunciad* and an index of the persons ridiculed: "twenty miles from London no body understands hints, initial letters, or town-facts and passages," and the poem, Swift thinks, will not be properly understood without them.[29] Both Augustans, one notices, are as far as can be from the lofty humanistic view that literature is a presentation of universal truths in universal language. Indeed, reading the *New Collection* is not very different in some respects from reading Mrs. Manley's notorious *New Atalantis.* Lust and scorn, scandal about people in high life, attacks on political and military leaders are plentiful in both books, although the *New Collection* has the virtue, if I may use the word, of presenting attacks on everybody, not just on Whigs. Pope's satires should be seen against the background of both Mrs. Manley's work and the *New Collection.* Only then will his literary discrimination, his finesse in personal satire, and the crispness and richness of his character-sketches stand out as they should.

What has been noticed about Pope's reading of the *New Collection* makes it harder for one to refrain from reading his poems in the same way—with pen in hand, jotting down names of individuals as they occur to one. Undoubtedly he expected one to do just that, at least with the *Dunciad,* the *Epistle to Lord Bathurst,* most of the

---

29. *Correspondence,* II, 504. Edward Harley also told Pope that several people had asked him for a key to the poem and he wishes "the True one was come out" (*Correspondence,* II, 496).

Horace, and the *Epilogue to the Satires.* His denial that the *Epistle to a Lady* contains portraits drawn from life indicates what he supposed the habits of readers, if not of writers, were. And when he hung up and pilloried by name certain individual banditti, he doubtless pleased many readers; moral indignation would be relieved, and admiration would be aroused for the poet's courage and force. A particular sinner—and many more like him, no doubt—had been checked for the good of the nation, and the sketch would be relished as a keen and witty account of what that egregious man's nature was.

CHAPTER III

POPE'S REVISION *of* CHARACTER-SKETCHES

A MONG the poets, Pope is the great editor. By 1735 it had become less than remarkable for writers to issue their own "Collected Works." But Pope's publishing a second volume of his *Works* in that year with footnotes that offered a collation of variant readings indicates not only his conception of his importance as an English author[1] but, further, his assumption that an examination of a good poet's several alternative phrasings is rewarding in itself. Many of Pope's poems were reprinted astonishingly often, and, as he anticipated, one now scans each subsequent edition for the modifications that his restless genius produced. Just as it is delightful and instructive to find Mr. Auden in an anthology of seventeenth- and eighteenth-century poetry[2] singling out for quotation from Thomson's *Seasons* a passage on the effect of "the vital Air" of spring on the conduct of birds that curiously enriches his own poignant poem on the physiology and psychology of that season,[3] so it is interesting to see Pope, as editor of Sheffield and "imitator" of Horace and Donne, busily tinkering with character-sketches in ways that are his own. What he did as he devotedly worked over these drawings and also those originated by himself should indicate something about his tastes in literature and his preferences in satire and panegyric.

---

1. John Butt, "Pope's Poetical Manuscripts," *Proceedings of the British Academy*, XL (1955), 23.

2. *Poets of the English Language. III. Milton to Goldsmith*, ed. W. H. Auden and Norman H. Pearson (New York, 1950), pp. 483-488.

3. "Spring 1940."

The changes he made in the more elaborate sketches demonstrate that he did not always move away from personal models or object to their being recognized. The large and showy picture of the inconsistent man called Clodio in the several early printings of the *Epistle to Lord Cobham* was frankly labeled Wharton in the "death-bed edition."[4] The more famous picture of Sporus—or Lord Hervey— was apparently added to the plan of the *Epistle to Dr. Arbuthnot* after most of the material for that poem was in shape.[5] Pope's multiple interlineations in a fair copy of the Sporus lines, now in the Morgan Library,[6] suggest that he labored hard over the sketch in order to make it just right. The array of vitriolic epithets he recorded here for his formerly accepted acquaintance may not be all he thought of; among those given, "pimp," "fool," "monkey," and "ape" did not find place in the final version. Monkeys and apes were images perhaps too harmless in suggestion, and "pimp" and "fool" would further have blurred the outline of the kind of evil creature Pope was trying to draw. These epithets were eliminated, one infers, because, though Pope probably meant in Sporus to attack all corrupt court-poets, he wished especially to create a carefully offensive portrait of Lord Hervey as a particular example.

How Pope could transform another author's material into an attack on one of his own *bêtes noires* can be seen in what he did with the

4. When I mention the "death-bed edition" I refer to the volume in the British Museum (shelf-mark C.59.e.1) which contains three parts: first, a quarto edition of *An Essay on Man. Being the First Book of Ethic Epistles . . . With the Commentary and Notes of Mr. Warburton. London, Printed for J. and P. Knapton . . . MDCCXLIII*; second, an undated quarto printing of *Epistles to Several Persons* (the epistles to Cobham, "To a Lady," to Bathurst, and to Burlington); third, an undated quarto printing of the *Essay on Criticism*. For further details see Bateson, pp. xiii-xv. Pope's letters to the printer Bowyer in February and March, 1743/44 (*Correspondence*, IV, 501-502, 504, 505, and notes) were presumably concerned with the printing and distributing of the editions of the *Essay on Man*, the *Essay on Criticism*, and *Epistles to Several Persons* represented in the volume in the British Museum. The date 1743 printed in the title-page of the *Essay on Man* may have been Old Style for a date early in 1744. The middle part of the volume (*Epistles to Several Persons*) would thus constitute the otherwise missing 1744 volume of *Epistles* that Pope presumably distributed just before he died; see Spence, p. 318, quoted above p. 3 n.

5. Butt, "Pope's Poetical Manuscripts," p. 37.

6. MS. MA. 352, fol. 7.

depiction of lawyers in Donne's second Satire. There were three stages in the process of adaptation.

In the original poem after a discursive opening Donne introduces a foolish young would-be poet, Coscus, who upon attaining the station of lawyer complacently speaks legal jargon even in wooing the ladies. Donne quotes samples of his grotesque language. Then, after an outburst against men who become lawyers only from greed, Donne proceeds to a somewhat meandering description of the lying rapacity of a lawyer who by dogged meanness and sly cheating will eventually possess all the land of England. One cannot be sure whether the remarks about this rapacious lawyer refer to Coscus in his later years, very much matured from foolish vanity into crime, or to someone else.

In an early, unpublished "translation" of Donne's poem made for Robert Harley Pope merely modernized the text line by line, though he also dropped the eight lines illustrating Coscus's absurd legal love-talk.[7] In this version the rapacious lawyer is set off more clearly from foolish Coscus.

In Pope's second version[8] a good many modifications occur. Donne's insolent young lawyer is now not only fop and ass but also criminal and wealthy, but his name (Coscus) is shifted to a second, newly invented rascal, a solemn-faced hypocrite who pretends to sacrifice himself for his clients while actually cheating them. Donne's complaint that the lawyer by his tricks will eventually grasp all the land of England is made into a third section in Pope's poem which assigns shocking behavior of that sort to "W**rs" (probably the notorious, powerful money-scrivener Peter Waters or Walter[9]) and other wicked lawyers.

In the first two printings of the poem such was the text provided. But in subsequent editions[10] the name "Peter" supplants "Coscus" as the label of the hypocritical cheater. Pope thus finally brings the

---

7. Both of Pope's versions of Donne are given in Butt, pp. 132-145.
8. In Pope's *Works, II* (1735), folio.
9. Butt, p. 392; *The Gentleman's Magazine*, XVI (1746), 45.
10. *Works,* II (1735), 8 vo., and later.

names "Peter" and "W**rs" into proximity; a well outlined caustic portrait, not in Donne, emerges for Peter Waters, and the attack on him is open and powerful. The fact that he is used as a known representative of a large, evil group does not at all blur the outlines of the individual portrait.

There was never any doubt about the subject of Pope's well-known picture of "Atticus." When this piece first appeared in print, possibly without permission, in *The St. James's Journal* (Dec. 15, 1722), the subject described was given as "Ad——n," and among the lines was a couplet about him—

> Who when two Wits on rival themes contest
> Approves them both, but likes the worst the best—

which doubtless would be understood by numerous readers as a reference to the quarrel over Pope's and Tickell's translations of Homer. When Pope many years later incorporated the portrait in the *Epistle to Dr. Arbuthnot*, the subject was called "Atticus" and the couplet about rival wits was omitted. Both changes render the sketch slightly more general, slightly less particularly about Addison. One might argue, however, that Pope dropped the allusion to the quarrel not so much to spare Addison as himself; revealing unabated rancor over that now-resolved competition would do Pope no honor. Actually, a footnote on this portrait when it was printed in the folio and quarto *Works* (1735) made perfectly clear that the line depicted a "Gentleman," now dead, whose identity was already known.

Two of Pope's most striking sketches underwent revisions that seem to produce a doubling of personal allusion in an especially tantalizing way. In each case was Pope trying to kill two birds with one stone? Or just one bird? Or was he trying rather to frighten a flock (a small flock) of offensive creatures?

> Proud, as Apollo on his forked hill,
> Sate full-blown Bufo, puff'd by ev'ry quill;
> Fed with soft Dedication all day long,
> Horace and he went hand in hand in song.

His Library, (where Busts of Poets dead
And a true Pindar stood without a head)
Receiv'd of Wits an undistinguish'd race,
Who first his Judgment ask'd, and then a Place:
Much they extoll'd the Pictures, much the Seat,
And flatter'd ev'ry day, and some days eat:
Till grown more frugal in his riper days,
He pay'd some Bards with Port, and some with Praise,
To some a dry Rehearsal was assign'd,
And others (harder still) he pay'd in kind.

(*An Epistle from Mr. Pope, to Dr. Arbuthnot,* 1734)

In a manuscript draft of this passage now in the Morgan Library the line just preceding this passage leaves the whole Parnassian state to "B-b," and in the lines themselves the subject is twice called "Bubo." It seems probable that Pope originally had George Bubb Dodington in mind and in the third and fourth lines alluded to Welsted's mentioning him instead of Maecenas in his paraphrase of Horace's first ode.[11] Other details fit Dodington well enough.

But when the poem was next printed (in the folio edition of Pope's *Works,* Volume Two, 1735), four lines were appended to the portrait of Bufo:

Dryden alone (what wonder?) came not nigh,
Dryden alone escap'd this judging eye:
But still the Great have kindness in reserve,
He help'd to bury him he help'd to starve.

These remarks could not apply to Dodington, who was only nine when Dryden died, but would instead shift the portrait to Charles Montague, Earl of Halifax, who was reported by more than one writer at the time of Dryden's death to have offered to erect a tomb for the poet he had once satirized.[12]

11. See Elwin-Courthope, III, 259 n.; Butt, pp. 112-113 n. Dodington's name had been George Bubb, but in 1720 on the death of a wealthy uncle who left him property he assumed the uncle's name.

12. *Prose Works of John Dryden,* ed. Edmond Malone (1800), I, i, 374-375 n., 383-384.

Tom Brown in *A Description of Mr. D——n's Funeral A Poem* (1700) wrote of Halifax

> He the great Bard at his own Charge Inters,
> And dying Vice to living Worth prefers.

Brown described Halifax as "sleek and fat," "as big as any Belgick Lord," gaining flatterers for himself as "the chief of Wits" by a distribution of gold to the wrong people. The vision evoked by Pope in the first ten lines in some respects matches Brown's and, in still more, the extraordinary account of Halifax ("Julius Sergius") which many of Pope's contemporaries must have seen in Mrs. Manley's *New Atalantis* and which, when seen, they were not likely to forget.[13] Sergius, having become "vain-glorious" as a tool of the government, is master of a prodigious fortune and keeps open-house in a sumptuous palace of joy and sensual pleasure. Because of his "great Interest" and power it was for a season "an absolute Fashion" to address oneself to him. He supposes himself therefore an excellent poet and a learned critic. His "Gallery is adorned with modern Pieces of Painting" of admirable dead and living leaders in the sciences and poetry, including (according to a 1720 "Key") Wycherley, Congreve, Addison, Prior, but not, one notices, Dryden or Pope. Sergius's dishonorable ingratitude toward Prior is deplored.

Pope's picture of Bufo includes much of this (though not the charge that Halifax encouraged debauchery), and it also reflects a current notion that he was covetous.[14] In the folio *Works* there is a footnote on the final line explaining that "by the contribution of several Persons of Quality" Dryden had been given a magnificent funeral; this note would doubtless have the effect of spreading the application of the sketch to "several Persons." Yet the self-indulgent,

---

13. *Secret Memoirs . . . of Several Persons of Quality . . . from the New Atalantis* (1720), III, 249-275.

14. Butt, p. 112 n. The argument (p. 113 n.) that these lines could not apply to Halifax because the fifteenth line suggests incorrectly that Dryden never applied to Bufo for favors is weak. Neither Pope nor his readers would be likely to know of Dryden's petition to Halifax for aid in 1699. As for line 8, Spence records Pope's saying that Halifax was rather "a pretender to taste, than really possessed of it" and then tells a fine story to illustrate the point; see Spence, pp. 134-136.

puffed-up, undiscriminating, rich, picture-collecting, stingy, unkind, vain man here depicted is a specialized variety of the literary patron. The laconic annotation by Pope's friend Edward Harley may again be trusted to state the case fairly: "this character made fit many but I think it is cheifly the right of Mr Bubb Doddington, it would also fitt the late earl of Halifax."[15]

The second instance of revision that defies simple classification as more personal or less personal in direction is the omission of a couplet from the sketch of Atossa. It introduces other questions about that much-debated piece which I postpone until a later chapter. But one aspect of the matter can be stated here. The couplet,

> Thus, while her Palace rises like a Town,
> Atossa cheats the Lab'rer of a crown,

was part of the account of Atossa when it was first printed.[16] In the death-bed text of the *Epistle to a Lady* and later editions this couplet is missing; readers would in consequence lose one very good hook with which to hang the portrait on the Duchess of Marlborough, whose troubles over costs when Blenheim Palace was building must have been known to many. But because of that omission readers would be more likely to identify the original—if they knew enough about her to do so—as the Duchess of Buckinghamshire.[17] The picture of Atossa was probably one of the sketches which Pope said he had omitted from the poem in its early form, and one could pardonably assume that Pope thought it so close a portrait of somebody that he dared not print it. The dropping of the couplet operates as did the addition of the last four lines to the picture of Bufo: though the intention may have been to widen the applicability of the sketch,

---

15. Bodleian Library shelf-mark M.3.19 Art.

16. In the text of the *Epistle to a Lady* in the apparently unique set of Pope's *Works* printed for the Prince of Wales about 1738. See Vinton A. Dearing, "The Prince of Wales's Set of Pope's Works," *Harvard Library Bulletin*, IV (1950), 320-338.

17. A good survey of the tangled evidence relating to the identification of Atossa can be found in Dearing's article, pp. 327-336. The only safe conclusion seems to be that Pope had each of the two duchesses in mind at one time or another as he worked on the passage.

the result is not only that but also a clearer possibility of individual, though shifted, portraiture. Such a paradox, such a double or even multiple vision, is one of the triumphant values produced by this busiest of revisers. One gets the impression, especially in such sketches as those of Cloe, Atossa, and Philomede (all added to the *Epistle to a Lady* in its late revisions), that Pope wished readers to have the excitement of suspecting the existence of particular, living originals without being able to fix the identification indisputably.

Something slightly different about Pope's revisions—a disinclination, when an opportunity presented itself, to reduce a complex, rare figure to a simple, universal type—can be seen in an interesting example.   Here is Sylvia, "A Fragment."

> Sylvia my Heart in wond'rous wise alarm'd,
> Aw'd without Sense, and without Beauty charm'd,
> But some odd Graces and fine Flights she had,
> Was just not ugly, and was just not mad:
> Her Tongue still run, on credit from her Eyes,
> More pert than witty, more a Wit than wise.[18]
> Good Nature, she declar'd it, was her Scorn,
> Tho' 'twas by that alone she could be born.
> Affronting all, yet fond of a good Name,
> A Fool to Pleasure, and a Slave to Fame:
> Now coy and studious in no Point to fall,
> Now all agog for D——y at a Ball:
> Now with a modest Matron's careful Air,
> Now her Fore Buttocks to the Navel bare.
> Now deep in Taylor and the Book of Martyrs,
> Now drinking Citron with his Gr— and Ch—
>
> Men, some to Business, some to Pleasure take,
> But ev'ry Woman's in her Soul a Rake.
> Frail, fev'rish Sex! their Fit now chills, now burns;
> Atheism and Superstition rule by Turns;

---

18. Dryden says the Buzzard (Burnet) was "More learn'd than Honest, more a Wit than learn'd" (*The Hind and the Panther*, III, 1150).

And the meer Heathen in her carnal Part,
Is still a sad good Christian at her Heart.[19]

This strange, impulsive, charming, astonishing creature may have been real. But if so, there is now no way of telling who she was, whether the Duchess of Hamilton or someone else,[20] and we must take her as she appears in these lively verses. Pope's amazement and fascination we share. Thinking of her at her best and worst we might in bewilderment conclude that "ev'ry Woman's in her Soul a Rake"; at least that remark is more appropriate here than in the *Epistle to a Lady* where Pope later put it and where it seems unnecessarily cynical.

What happened when Pope broke up the portrait of Sylvia and made from it, with two couplets to spare, both Calypso and Narcissa in the *Epistle to a Lady?* To Calypso he assigned Sylvia's oddity of manner and appeal, "just not ugly" and "just not mad." Less amazing than Sylvia, Calypso is less vivid because there are no particular statements, as there are in the earlier picture, to suggest what her flights are or why, without virtue or beauty or wisdom or wit, she awes and charms. She is still not a recognizable type, nor is her individuality so striking as Sylvia's.

To Narcissa Pope assigned the specific illustrations of Sylvia's wildness, the Martyrs-Chartres couplet, and the carnal good-Christian contradiction that in the "Fragment" belonged to all women. To the flutter of antitheses taken over from the earlier poem Pope adds others intensifying the tone of disapproval.[21] The psychological make-up of Narcissa is more baffling than that of Sylvia. Sylvia "affronts" all; so her disavowal of good nature at the same time that she seeks approbation ("a slave to Fame") is no more contradictory than the rest of the conduct of this modest matron naked to the navel. But Narcissa is not so bizarre and not, as Sylvia and Calypso are, nearly mad. She "piques" everybody instead of affronting them; spared the

---

19. *Miscellanies. The Last Volume*, pp. 136-137.
20. Bateson, pp. 52-53 n.; Ault and Butt, p. 287 n.
21. See pp. 51-52 below for a parallel in Law to one feature given to Narcissa.

coarsest line,[22] she seems more decorous, more conventional. But Pope makes her more difficult to understand when he says that she is utterly hard-hearted, a feature not easy to imagine in one whom alternately "Conscience chills" and "Passion burns." Furthermore, Sylvia seems not to have been deliberately dishonest or otherwise immoral as Calypso and Narcissa are. These three sketches cannot be evaluated as portraits of individual women whom Pope knew, for one cannot be sure of the originals. As a description of the manners and a divination into the nature of a possible, curious human being, the picture of Sylvia is much the best. For all her contradictions she is more plausible and real than the two derived ladies. But as fantastic illustrations of self-contradiction, Calypso and Narcissa serve well enough. Inconsistency may be universal though the natures of these ladies are not.

The most surprising modification Pope made in any of his character-sketches occurs in the text of the *Epistle to a Lady* as it appears in the set of his *Works* which he made up for presentation to the Prince of Wales, probably in 1738. In the first edition of the poem (1735) Pope invites the reader to

> look on Simo's Mate,
> No Ass so meek, no Ass so obstinate,

and then with similar brevity he calls attention to three other women, the "honest" one who refuses to improve herself, the lady "whose Life the Church and Scandal share," and the unstrung, maudlin lady addicted to opium and ratafia. A fifth lady, "who laughs at Hell," was added to the group when the poem appeared later in the year in the quarto edition of the *Works*. But very different is the passage as it was printed in the Prince of Wales's copy:

> Turn then from Wits to Issachar's dull Mate,
> No Ass so meek, no Ass so obstinate:
> True, that's her fault, and faults she never mends
> Because she's honest, and the best of Friends.

---

22. The "Fore Buttocks" line Pope tried out again in the 1728 editions of *Dunciad* II and then placed permanently in *Sober Advice from Horace* (1734).

See what a sweet Vicissitude appears
Of Mirth and Opium, Ratafie and Tears!
The daily Anodyne and nightly draught,
To kill those foes to Fair ones, Time and Thought.
At Hell she laughs; but like her simple Grace
Cries, O! how charming if there's no such place![23]

Thus four of the five hastily but clearly differentiated women are compounded into one woman who is far from clear and much less a type. "The method makes one wonder how frequently Pope's characters may have come into being by mere synthesis or accretion rather than by development from traits in a single person."[24] Apparently Pope (or Warburton?) saw his mistake: in the death-bed edition the passage was restored to what it had been in the quarto *Works.*

In the course of his long career Pope became the most eminent of neo-classical writers; so his revision of classical character-sketches should prove interesting. His admiration for Homer's "Distinction of Characters" and his praise for Andromache's lament as containing "nothing general in her Sorrows" indicate the bent of his theory. Further revelation comes in a note on an earlier scene in Homer— Hector's moment with Andromache when the fright of their babe at Hector's glittering helmet requires Hector to remove it before lifting the infant toward the skies (VI, 595-621). There never was, comments Pope,

a finer Piece of Painting than this. . . . All these are but small Circumstances, but so artfully chosen, that every Reader immediately feels the force of them, and represents the whole in the utmost Liveliness to his Imagination. This alone might be a Confutation of that false Criticism some have fallen into, who affirm that a Poet ought only to collect the great and noble Particulars in his Paintings. But it is in the Images of Things as in the Characters of Persons; where a small Action, or even a small Circumstance of an Action, lets us more into the Knowledge and

---

23. The Prince of Wales's copy of Pope's *Works,* II (a 1737 title-page), in the Harvard College Library, shelf-mark 15443.1717.5*.
24. Dearing, "The Prince of Wales's Set of Pope's Works," p. 326.

Comprehension of them, than the material and principal Parts themselves. As we find this in a History, so we do in a Picture, where sometimes a small Motion or Turning of a Finger will express the Character and Action of the Figure more than all the other Parts of the Design. . . .

The apt, perhaps small, but specific detail for the distinguishing of characters is what one expects Pope to value, and in his revisions one may look for modifications of this sort.

An early example is the lively picture of the bookful-blockhead critic presented in the third section of the *Essay on Criticism*. A footnote in the first edition acknowledges a source by quoting in full Quintilian's less vivid description (I, i, 8) of the conduct of ignorant, arrogant slave-tutors. Changing some of the essentials of the figure, Pope also embroiders freely and brightly: his offender is a mad, abandoned critic with "Loads of Learned Lumber in his Head," who attacks all that he reads, "From Dryden's Fables down to D——y's Tales," and who accuses Garth of not having written *The Dispensary*, pretends to be an adviser to playwrights, and pours out ceaseless nonsense wherever he goes. Though the added details are not so delicate as the "Turning of a Finger," they are definite and expressive.

A similar enlivening by means of particular detail and more clearly differentiated persons occurs in Pope's remodeling of a passage in Horace's first Epistle. This is the somewhat unexpected short discussion of the incorrigible unsteadiness and inconsistency of that lesser Proteus, man. Impelled by caprice, a fellow will move from Baiae to Teanum; if married he envies the bachelor, and if single he longs for the happiness of the husband. Even the man who is poor changes his garrets, his couches, his barber. Horace rushes over these illustrations of his thesis without making any of his supposed people very definite; he wants, rather, to give an impression of constant flux as normal.

Pope's version, twice as long as Horace's, not only brightens the illustrations with a-la-mode references to Greenwich and Thames, japanner, sculler, a chaise, and the spleen; it also shapes the hypothetical possibilities into figures that are more distinct—Sir Job and his lady, "am'rous Flavio," a Fool who is a cuckold, and a more exactly described group of "the Poor." The idea of human caprice and change remains, but Pope gives the reader a more tangible vision of the separate individuals that make up the busy population of the world.

In a third case Pope's modification of the material in a Latin original goes beyond clearer outline of representative figures to the "Knowledge and Comprehension" of an individual person. This is the appealing sketch in *Windsor Forest* of Pope's early friend and mentor, Sir William Trumbull, portrayed in the role of wise and happy country gentleman. The groundwork, the "allusion," for the literary pattern here was undoubtedly the passage at the end of the second Book of the *Georgics*,[25] where Vergil somewhat casually sketches, one after another, the fortunate life of the real farmer; the poet's own dream of becoming a profound student of stars, earth, and sea; his alternative vision of a mostly sensuous joy in nature; the happiness of the Lucretian philosopher; and again the enviable independence of the sturdy farmer who gives no time to politics, warfare, or city corruptions. In the 1712 manuscript version of *Windsor Forest*[26] Pope adapted this material in a fourteen-line paragraph which was almost doubled in length for the printed version of 1713. In the latter text Pope abandoned Vergil's several type-images and evoked a different vision of a life and a character richer and more complex than any in the Latin poem. Numerous specific facts about the retired man's studies (mineral chemistry, "ancient writ," history, medicinal herbs), the "small Circumstance" of his daily routine ("Successive study, exercise, and ease"), and his moral philosophy and religious faith make this Pope's most elaborate and detailed portrait. If not so subtly searching as the familiar one of Addison, it is none the less an excellent full-length picture. To be sure, it catches its subject only at a late point in his career and misses some features

25. See Elwin-Courthope, I, 354-355 n., for minor debts to other sources.

26. See *Pope's Windsor Forest 1712 A Study of the Washington University Holograph*, ed. Robert M. Schmitz (St. Louis, Mo., 1952). In this text the sketch is ll. 236-249.

of character—cowardice, for instance—that earlier contemporaries of Trumbull complained about.[27] Instead an aura of idealism flatteringly suffuses the lines, partly from Pope's gratitude to his friendly mentor and partly, no doubt, because of the eloquent, even at times ecstatic tone of Vergil's sketching. One cannot say as Pope did of Andromache's lament that there is nothing general here, for phases of Europe's finest tradition of civilized living are being recalled. But the portrait is individualized beyond any part of Vergil's passage.

In each of the three examples just surveyed, modernization has transformed a classical picture into something more particular.[28] Images of individuals come to mind more readily. On the contrary, in two other cases—the brief descriptions of Walsh at the end of the *Essay on Criticism* and of Bolingbroke at the end of the *Essay on Man*[29]—Pope's adaptation of classical material produced no increase in particularity or vividness; the pictures, both complimentary in intention, are general and obviously incomplete.

In still another pair of sketches the addition of specific detail creates a special effect. Horace's second satire in Book One presents the usurer Fufidius, who is eager for victims and remorseless when he captures them. He is just what one would expect an evil usurer to be. But in Pope's *Sober Advice from Horace* Fufidius becomes the woman Fufidia, still given to usury but in addition as shamelessly and insatiably carnal as she is greedy and cruel. She is less universal than Horace's figure, more peculiar and revolting and *outrée*. Another of Horace's sketches of parsimonious types, Avidienus in the second satire in Book Two, supplies, as his picture of Fufidius does, the expected details (of clothes and food in this case) to reveal a familiar type. Pope adds the unusual feature to Avidienus and his

27. See Pepys's slurs as quoted in the article on Trumbull in *DNB*.

28. Another adaptation, Pope's angry lines about the false friend based upon Horace's picture of the backbiter (*Sat.*, I, iv, 81-85), shows in a more limited way his particularizing an ancient type-sketch. First published in the *London Evening Post*, Jan. 22-25, 1732, and later incorporated in the *Epistle to Dr. Arbuthnot*, the English version shapes the type to fit those among Pope's acquaintances who said that Timon's villa in the *Epistle to Lord Burlington* ridiculed Lord Chandos's estate, Cannons.

29. See below, pp. 73-74.

wife of their being joyful over the death of their son. The modification in these cases suggests the influence of Juvenal, who, for instance, at the end of his terrifying account of the wicked proclivities of women, tells us that a wife will sometimes destroy her husband's illegitimate children out of hatred or a ward in order to gain his estate (VI, 627-633). Elsewhere (XIV, 220-228) in a sermon on the importance of parental example Juvenal warns that in imitation of an avaricious father a son might murder his wife for her dowry. In both passages the poet's fearful earnestness prepares one for horrible illustrations. In the monotone of Pope's account of the avaricious parents, the mention of their pleasure in their son's drowning comes with a shock. Avidien and his wife are not just misers; they are monsters. The alterations in both of these sketches have been attributed to a desire on Pope's part to lash out at Lady Mary Wortley Montagu and her husband; but whether so or not, they show Pope limiting the representativeness of a classical type. In the grossness and horror of the specific additions one sees him transforming Horace into Juvenal.

That Pope like Horace sometimes reaches Juvenalian intensity is beyond question.[30] Pope and Horace could also be as lavish with particular and sensory detail as Juvenal, but such writing is not so likely to occur in Horace's character-sketches as in Juvenal's and Pope's. One observes, too, that the frequency with which Pope places brightly realized sketches in several of his poems has a plainer precedent in Juvenal (II and VI) and Martial than in Horace. Nor did Horace compose as many recognizable portraits of prominent contemporaries as Pope did. Even when the identity of the subject of one of Pope's individualized drawings cannot be positively named, the reader's mind is often impelled to infer the existence of a particular model. This perpetual vividness, this ever-reviving suggestiveness of the tangible actualities of contemporary life, is an important ele-

---

30. See Reuben A. Brower, *Alexander Pope The Poetry of Allusion* (Oxford, 1959), p. 179. G. K. Hunter points out that in adapting Horace's first satire in Book Two Pope shifts from Horace's generally sympathetic view of the state to a hostility that is characteristic of Juvenal; see "The Romanticism of Pope's Horace," *Essays in Criticism*, X (1960), 393.

ment in the power of the satires. In some cases—Clodio, Atticus, Bufo, Peter, Sporus—a well-aimed gun has been fired, and the reader in the midst of applause shudders at the fatality.

Besides Pope's delight in animating detail and individualizing elaboration we should notice that he valued neatness and firmness of design in pen-portraits, the setting off of most of them as distinctly as a stone bust in a garden. This is especially clear in his transformation of Donne's perpetually tangential presentation of Coscus and in his building up the figure of the happy country-dweller out of Vergil's somewhat piecemeal depiction of several kinds of people. Pope often printed the original texts of Donne and Horace facing his modernization so that the curious reader would recognize and no doubt admire his transformations. But the extensive revision he gave to Sheffield's well-known *Essay upon Satyr* was not printed in that way and seems not to have been often noticed.

Sheffield's poem opened discursively. Then after a view of King Charles's mistresses, damned together as "False, foolish, old, ill-natur'd, and ill bred," it offered a remarkable set of seven portraits— of Buckingham (Villiers), Shaftesbury, Halifax (Savile), Heneage Finch, Dorset, Sheffield himself, and Sedley, each drawn in about twenty lines and in a bold, easy manner as if by a personal acquaintance. Although the treatment is not always gentle, only one of these accounts, that of Finch, is entirely hostile. After the series of seven portraits comes something which is really savage, Sheffield's picture of the Earl of Rochester, with whom he had bitterly quarreled. This forty-line passage condemns the man as lewd, cowardly, malicious, and his poetry as nasty, without wit, and worthless.

When Pope prepared the poem for inclusion in his handsome edition of Sheffield's *Works* (1723), he made various minor changes, deleting an obscenity in one sketch and an obscure personal detail in the lines on Sheffield. But the portrait of Rochester he handled freely. Though the man is still lewd and a coward, Pope says that "his very Vices shine," and represents him not as in "want of wit" and "affected in his Wit" as Sheffield had done but, on the contrary, as "of sprightly Wit." The last fourteen lines of the original sketch dealing with Rochester's poetry are dropped. Thus the evaluation of Rochester's talent is quite different from what Sheffield intended. By his bold alterations Pope produced a sketch similar to the other seven in length, in tone, and, since none of them now includes literary criticism, in subject matter. A more harmonious, better proportioned picture-gallery results, with the regularity, let us say, of Kneller's Kit-Kat series instead of the sometimes disorderly variation in size of the paintings on the wall of a Hogarth interior. When, a dozen years later, Pope created his own collection of paintings for his *Epistles* he allowed himself much more variety in size of sketch and in mood than he had permitted to Sheffield.

The modifications of the portrait of Rochester are unusual for Pope in that they reduce the amount of distinguishing and graphic detail[31] (though not the complexity of the character) and moderate the hatefulness of the figure. But characteristically the revision satisfies a taste for density in a picture. By adding sprightly wit and a glossy manner to a man whom Sheffield represents as a dull, lewd, base, cringing coward, Pope probably made a truer portrait of the famous gentleman and poet as well as reshaping the image of a recognizable type into something a little more unusual.[32]

The evidence thus suggests several conclusions about Pope. Though he liked to isolate one figure from another in the revisions we have examined, he did not usually do so by setting them off as simple—or simplified—types. Variety, intricacy, eccentric and circumstantial manifestations of inner motives seem to have appealed to his imagination at least as much as significant repetition in man's nature. Generality in a picture, however classical its authority, he tended to dissipate by painting in particular details. Whether he was utilizing

---

31. The following lines are omitted:
   To every face he cringes while he speaks,
   But when the back is turn'd, the head he breaks.

32. Another of Pope's efforts to improve a character-sketch written by someone else—his revising, at her request, the Duchess of Buckinghamshire's sketch of herself—cannot be examined. The lady's manuscript seems not to have survived, and there is no certainty that Pope was responsible for *The Character of Katharine, Late Duchess of Buckinghamshire and Normanby. By the late Mr. Pope* (1746).

material in sketches by earlier writers or revising his own, his sensibility guided him in satire towards an individualized representation. He provokes thought about human nature and human ideals by attracting the reader's mind to present, special cases.

CHAPTER IV

DERIVATIONS *and* DEVELOPMENTS

Pope's Sketches *in* Relation *to*
Earlier Sketches *of the* Same
or Similar Subjects

URING the mornings in 1713 when Pope was studying painting under Charles Jervas's tutelage he concentrated on portraits.
He made several efforts at paintings of Swift and of Lady Bridgewater, and he attempted a few sacred subjects as well as the Queen,
the Duchess of Montagu, and various noblemen. At least so it seems
from the comical reports he sent to his friends.[1] Spence states that
he had seen "of Mr. Pope's drawing, a grave old Chaucer, from
Occleve; a Betterton; a Lucius Verus, large profile; two Turkish
heads; a Janizary from the life; Antinous; and St. John praying."[2]

Jervas professed the greatest devotion to Lady Bridgewater, one
of the beautiful daughters of the Duke of Marlborough, and Pope
may have had an occasional glimpse of her as well as Jervas's painting (or paintings) to guide him. In his attempts to depict Swift he
presumably worked from Jervas's portrait, made as early as 1709-10.
Swift was not in London at the time Pope mentioned his failures in
painting him. Spence's note indicates that Pope sometimes drew from
the life and sometimes copied other artists' work. The portrait of
Betterton, who had died in 1710, is a remarkably good copy of
Kneller's painting of the actor, departing from it only in the color
of the wig and also slightly in facial expression. Perhaps this picture

---

1. *Correspondence*, I, 177, 187, 189.
2. Spence, p. 336.

is the "masterpiece" of his that he once referred to.[3] The Chaucer, based upon the well-known one in the precious Occleve manuscript, may possibly have been drawn in the library of Pope's friends, the Harleys. The interesting question for us is whether when he copied pictures Pope followed the originals exactly or whether he departed significantly from his predecessors' work in composition or technique or style. In the case of the Betterton the variation is slight but interesting; the face presented by Pope lacks something of the genial and elegant self-assurance that Kneller's painting reveals. But whether this difference was due to a deliberate effort on Pope's part to be true to his recollection of his friend's face and personality or whether it was an accidental result of his workmanship—or even the effect of time and dirt on the canvas—one cannot say. Nor could one depend upon this particular example to represent what Pope always did.

Ut pictura poesis? We have seen that in reshaping the imaginary figures that he found in Horace, Donne, and Quintilian Pope worked with complete freedom, transforming the originals to suit his purposes. Sheffield's strong portrait of his hated contemporary, the Earl of Rochester, came out in Pope's edition of Sheffield a curiously changed affair. Several of the historical figures portrayed in Pope's own poems and of course many of the types had already been presented in literary form—in satire or biography or Character-books, not to stray farther into drama and prose-fiction; it should be interesting to see how his sketches compare with the previous ones. Just as many of his best poems may be admired as modern adaptations of ancient genres, so his character-sketches may be examined as literary experiments with traditional subjects and with older techniques.

In the present chapter a selection of material is offered comparing certain of Pope's sketches with earlier ones of the same or similar subjects. It is hoped that this material, taken with that presented in the previous chapter, will cast some new light on Pope's interests and on the use he could make of literary precedents. This material will emphasize, more than his revisions do, the traditional element in his work. There is the difficulty, however, that often one cannot be sure

---

3. See Appendix A.

which precedent, if any, served as a model. Not all the parallels I have assembled are close. Indeed I should in many cases be willing to surrender the resemblance to mere accident or to the not very surprising fact that living models and literary models may supply identical inspiration. But even in the cases where no indebtedness can be proved, Pope's location in his own world, social, moral, and literary, should become a little clearer.

i. Sketches of Types

Certain ancient types Pope preserved plain and recognizable. Though he gave to his miser in the *Epistle to Lord Bathurst* the name that belonged to a bountiful giver, Cotta, in Juvenal's fifth Satire (perhaps to start the irony that expands so flauntingly in the succeeding picture of Cotta's son), Pope portrayed the miser in a familiar way, living in a great dilapidated estate denying food to his dog as to his tenants. *Outré* additions such as he made to Horace's miserly Avidienus and Fufidius do not mar the design of character. The flower-fancier in *Dunciad* Book Four plainly reminds one of Florio (in Edward Young's second Satire) who worships his Paul Diack tulip and of La Bruyère's *fleuriste* (the original of Young's) who adores a tulip called "solitaire."[4] The sexual imagery in Pope's sketch, comically accentuated in a footnote-reference to Catullus, does not seriously modify the type; neither does the shift from tulip to a carnation named Caroline.[5]

An ancient and appealing type, twice revived by Pope, is that of the happy country-dweller. Roman poets liked to dream about him. Whether they visualized this happy figure ("beatus," "felix," "for-

---

4. *Tatler* No. 218 had laughed at tulip-fanciers and the magnificent names they gave to various species of "these gay vegetables."

5. Just following Pope's picture of the flower-fancier comes his account of the man who ruined the carnation because of his devotion to the insect that lighted on it—"this peerless butterfly." In the chapter "De la Mode" in La Bruyère's *Caractères* about a dozen paragraphs later than the *fleuriste* is an account of a lover of insects ("c'est surtout le premier homme de l'Europe pour les papillons"), which ends in the admiring phrase, "quelle chenille."

tunatus") as a hardy farmer cheerfully engaged in rural labor[6] or, instead, as a gentleman retiring to the country to be a quiet spectator of its beauty,[7] they placed him in a kind of Golden Age; the innocence of his life was lauded in contrast to the strife and greedy ambition and worldliness of the city.

For a hundred years before Pope, English writers also had been celebrating the life of simple country retirement. Sometimes cheerful and active, sometimes Il Penseroso, sometimes a man abstractedly having green thoughts in a green shade, and sometimes, especially during the Restoration, a gentleman anticipating a much less spiritual gratification in a flowery retreat, the "happy man" kept reappearing in literature to offer his rebuke to the madding crowd.[8] The Roman poets and moralists provided the pattern; turbulent times and the benevolence of the English climate to the gardener made it steadily plausible.

Pope's "Ode on Solitude," written he said when he was "not Twelve years old," offers a wistful version of the image. The text as Pope sent it to a friend in 1709 is as follows:

> Happy the Man, who free from Care,
> The Business and the Noise of Towns,
> Contented breaths his Native Air,
> In his own Grounds:

> Whose Herds with Milk, whose Fields with Bread,
> Whose Flocks supply him with Attire,
> Whose Trees in Summer yield him Shade,
> In Winter, Fire.

> Blest, who can unconcern'dly find
> His Years slide silently away,

---

6. Vergil, *Georgics*, II, 458-460, 500-502, 513-531; Horace, Epode II; Claudian, "De sene Veronensi."

7. *Georgics*, II, 485-489; Horace, *Sat.*, II, vi; *Epist.*, I, x and xvi; Martial, V, xx; X, xlvii and xcvi; and the ascribed epigram, "Rure morans quid agam."

8. Maren-Sofie Rostvig has splendidly surveyed the whole subject in her two volumes, *The Happy Man: Studies in the Metamorphoses of a Classical Ideal*, I (Oslo and Oxford, 1954); II (Oslo and New York, 1958).

> In Health of Body, Peace of Mind,
> > Quiet by Day,
>
> Repose at Night; Study & Ease,
> Together mixt; sweet Recreation;
> And Innocence, which most does please,
> > With Meditation.
>
> Thus, let me live, unseen, unknown,
> > Thus, unlamented, let me die,
> Steal from the World, & not a Stone
> > Tell where I lye.[9]

Such a blending of agricultural self-sufficiency, ease, and studious meditation would be hard to find in the ancient poets' descriptions of the ideal life. Instead the combination indicates Pope's awareness of the English modification of the Roman pattern. This he could have seen exemplified in innumerable places, including Dryden's Dedication of his translation of the *Georgics*, where it is asserted—falsely—that Vergil seemed to think a country life insufficient without books. More important for Pope undoubtedly was an anthology of material on the subject of the "happy man" provided in four essays by Abraham Cowley.

Cowley's essay "Of Agriculture" explicated the *Georgics* faithfully and emphasized Vergil's idea of the satisfaction to be derived from living on the produce of one's own labor. At the end of the essay Cowley provided translations of several relevant Latin texts, including the finale of *Georgics* Book Two, Horace's second Epode, and his tenth Epistle. Among Pope's early exercises was an imitation of Cowley called "The Garden," and the young poet may in part have been drawn to his famous predecessor in precocity by his devotion to the *beatus ille* theme. Certainly Pope could have obtained all the material he needed for the "Ode" from Cowley's "Of Agriculture," supplemented by his essays "Of Solitude" and "The Garden" (to which translations of Martial, X, xlvii and xcvi, were appended) and "The dangers of an Honest man in much Company" (to which a

9. *Correspondence*, I, 68-69.

translation of Claudian's "Old Man of Verona" was appended). But the form of Pope's poem resembles the design of the "precept-Character" in verse composed in England in the early seventeenth century.[10]

His second utilization of the type of the "happy man," the passage in *Windsor Forest* depicting Sir William Trumbull in retirement, has already been discussed as an illustration of Pope's tendency to accumulate particularizing detail.[11] It is worth noticing also for its evolution out of several ancient patterns into a special new one. In the *Georgics* the description of the sturdy farmer's life was separate from the pictures of the delighted spectator of nature and the studious poet-philosopher, all three patterns being contrasted with the vexatious lives of sailors, warriors, the rich, the ambitious. In the 1712 manuscript draft of *Windsor Forest* Pope hastily alludes to the country-lover and the poet but proposes, as more blessed than either, the man who, retired to the country, is a seeker after both scientific and moral knowledge. Love of nature is much less prominent in Pope's sketch than it is in various parts of the long passage in Vergil; substituted for that feeling is a new spirituality in the man's study of the stars, apparently based upon Trumbull's own life.[12] Vergil's conclusion about the bucolic happiness of the Sabines and Romulus and Remus is gracefully adapted by Pope:

> Such was the Life great Scipio once admir'd;
> Thus Atticus, and Trumball thus retir'd.

In the expanded version of the portrait for the 1713 printed text, additional details about the man's studies give him a more modern

---

10. See my *Theophrastan Character in England to 1642* (Cambridge, Mass., 1947), pp. 94-96.

11. See above, pp. 36-37.

12. For confirmation of the propriety of painting Trumbull as one who "Bids his free soul expatiate in the skies" see Pope's letter to him (Dec. 16, 1715) in which he writes: "I sincerely wish my self with you, to contemplate the wonders of God in the firmament, rather than the madness of man on the earth" (*Correspondence*, I, 324). Earl R. Wasserman (*The Subtler Language* [Baltimore, 1959], pp. 144-150) sees this passage as a deliberately contrived exposition, without reference to Vergil, of the proper progress of the soul toward civilized excellence.

look, and some echoing of Dryden's free translation of Vergil's passage accentuates his spiritual preoccupation.[13] Yet in spite of the many
new and personal features the picture is recognizably of the ancient
type and eloquently renews its ideal. The connoisseur will take his
choice, preferring either the attractive pale tints and generality of
the "Ode" that crystallizes a century's wistfulness, or the highly
wrought, gracefully synthetic piece of hortatory portraiture in *Windsor Forest.*

The account of Timon in the *Epistle to Lord Burlington* now
seems peculiarly Pope's creation, especially because of our knowledge
of the allegation that in him Pope deliberately incorporated insulting
resemblances to the Duke of Chandos. That there are in the picture
actual reflections of what Pope had heard about or seen in certain
great mansions of the day must of course be assumed. Yet Timon is
also Pope's lavish variation on an ancient literary theme. There had
been Cretonius in Juvenal's Satire Fourteen, who threw away vast
sums on the construction of villa after villa, each ornamented like
Timon's hall with imported marble. After Cretonius's death what
money was left his son exhausted on the erection of more marble
villas. There was in La Bruyère's *Caractères* the bourgeois who built
a mansion so beautiful that it was, for a bourgeois, uninhabitable;[14]

---

13. Compare the following lines in the character-sketch in *Windsor Forest* (1713)
with lines from the passage, not so compact, in Dryden: (*a*) "Whom humbler Joys of
home-felt Quiet please" and Dryden (657): " With homebred Plenty the rich Owner
bless," a line freely expanded from Vergil's "Dives opum variarum" (468). Pope
combined Dryden's phrase and "secura quies" from the previous line in Vergil. (*b*)
"Now marks the Course of rolling Orbs on high" and Dryden (677): "Give me the
Ways of wandring Stars to know," a line amplifying the Latin "caelique vias et sidera
monstrent." (*c*) "Or looks on Heav'n with more than mortal Eyes,/ Bids his free Soul
expatiate in the Skies" and Dryden (685-688): "But if my heavy Blood restrain
the Flight/ Of my free Soul, aspiring to the Height/ Of Nature, and unclouded Fields
of Light." Vergil's single line from which Dryden's three were developed speaks only
of being barred from reaching certain realms of nature ("Sin, has ne possim naturae
accedere partis").

14. *Les Caracteres de Theophraste* . . . *Avec les Caracteres ou les Moeurs de
ce Siecle, Par M. de la Bruyere,* 3 vols. (Amsterdam, 1720), I, 406. This edition is
the one which Pope cited as his source for a quotation in "The Publisher to the
Reader" in the first edition of the *Dunciad* (1728). Unless otherwise identified, all
references to La Bruyère's *Caractères* will be to this edition.

and in the collection of La Bruyère's imitator Brillon there was the rich Atale whose house was so vast that the visitor would wander through hall after hall without finding the owner, hidden in a remote apartment.[15] Timon's "building is a Town," and Brillon thinks Atale might as well live in the Louvre. In Mandeville's *Fable of the Bees* (1714), Remark O, one is told about the "wordly-minded, voluptuous and ambitious Man" who, desiring to be dignified above his betters, "aims at spacious Palaces, and delicious Gardens," and all the ornaments of a magnificent estate. In William Law's *Practical Treatise upon Christian Perfection* (1726) one meets Siccus, a man without virtues or vices who "has been all his life-long building and pulling down, making Canals and Ditches, raising Walls and Fences: People call him a good Man, because he employs the Poor; Siccus might have been a religious Man, but that he thought building was the chief Happiness of a rational Creature."[16] In Edward Young's first Satire there is Belus, who

> Sinks in a Quarry an immense Estate;
> In Cost and Grandeur Ch—dos he'll out-do,
> And, B—l——ton, thy Taste is not so true.[17]

But Belus hides in a corner of the mansion to avoid his bills. Just beside him in Young's poem is Pygmalion, whose heart and fortune go into antique statues while his daughter starves. These various men are not entirely alike, but they illustrate the love of great mansions and cold display. Pope's adaptation of the tradition in Timon was for his own purpose; a well-read contemporary would have recognized the venerability as well as the modernity of the figure and would have relished, no doubt, the conjunction of literature and life in this essay on contemporary taste. The visual quality that distinguishes Pope's treatment from all the others will be remarked upon later.

---

15. *Le Theophraste Moderne* (1700), p. 190. Brillon's work was printed in Volumes II and III of the 1720 Amsterdam edition of La Bruyère. Atale appears there in III, 31.

16. Pp. 296-297.

17. *The Universal Passion. Satire I* (1725), p. 11.

There are a number of subjects in Pope's gallery who seem much odder than Timon; yet for them too there were literary precedents. Such is Flavia in the first edition of the *Epistle to a Lady* (Sappho in the third and later editions) whose diamonds agree badly with her dirty smock and whose "self in glue (her rising task)" fails to foretell her appearance later "issuing fragrant to an evening Mask." But one is not surprised by Flavia if one has read about the rich wife in Juvenal's sixth Satire (ll. 461-473) whose face at home with her husband is covered with sticky grease and plaster but is clean when she meets her adulterous lover. In a later edition Pope changed the words about "glue" to "her toilet's greazy task," thus blurring slightly the resemblance to Juvenal. Annotators have often supposed that Flavia-Sappho was one more insulting picture of Lady Mary Wortley Montagu, notorious in later life for untidiness and notable for the habit, according to Horace Walpole, of endeavoring to conceal the pock-marks in her face by filling up the depressions with white paint.[18] Regardless of Lady Mary, Flavia-Sappho was not the first of her kind.

Papillia in the *Epistle to a Lady* is a special case (with some of the odium distributed to her "am'rous Spark") of the changeable female frequently depicted by earlier writers. Boileau speaks of

> la Fantasque inégale,
> Qui m'aimant le matin, souvent me hait le soir.[19]

Richard Flecknoe's Character of a "Changeable disposition" represents at tedious length a woman who is now stormy, now sunny, now merry, now sad, "now infinitly obligeing, & as disobliging now again. Whence who observe her humour are tyred out and become giddy strait."[20] Another of Flecknoe's Characters, the "Fantastique Lady," renders several of Pope's strange women recognizable, and I quote all of it:

---

18. Sir James Prior, *Life of Edmond Malone* (1860), pp. 149-150.

19. Satire X, 662-663. Bibula in Juvenal (VI) resembles Papillia in making insatiable demands on a doting husband.

20. *Enigmaticall Characters, All Taken to the Life* (1658), pp. 90-91.

Her life is a perpetuall contradiction, she would and she would not, and make ready the Coach, yet let it alone too; drive to such a place, yet do not neither; Is her ordinary dialect: she differs from the irresolute, in that he is alwayes beginning, and she never makes an end; she writes and blots out again, whilest he deliberates what to write: t'on being a resty, tother a restless pain: so you can tell what to make of ton's Negative, and how two Negatives make an Affirmative; but of her *I* and *no* together, you know not what to make, but only that she knows not what to make of it her self. Her head is just like a Mill, or Squirrels cage, and her minde the Squirrel that turns and whirls it round,[21] and her imagination differs from others, as your Grotesque figures do from naturall and from grotesque; In that these have some design in them, but her imagination has none: She never looking towards the end, but onely the beginning of things; or if she does, forgets or disapproves it strait: For she will call in all hast for one, and have nothing to say to him when he is come; and long (nay dye) for some toy or trifle, which having once, she grows weary of presently, and throws away.[22] In fine, who are of one minde to day, and another to morrow, are constant to her, and Saturns revolution compared unto the Moons; For you know not where to have her a moment, and whosoever would hit her thoughts must shoot flying; and fly themselves whosoever would follow her.[23]

This sketch, though much too ample for Pope, reminds one of the contradictory natures of his Papillia, Atossa, and Narcissa. Its penultimate remark that "whosoever would hit her thoughts must shoot flying" resembles Pope's observation on the problem of painting such fantastics: "Some flying Stroke, alone can hit them right."

Narcissa, the peculiar lady partly created from Pope's earlier picture of Sylvia, becomes less strange in her whims and in her hardheartedness (a feature not derived from Sylvia) after one encounters a woman William Law had recently described in *A Serious Call to a Devout and Holy Life* (1729). This is Flavia, a self-centered, irreligious, churchgoing lady of fashion who makes a fine figure on a

---

21. Atossa's busy mind is similar:
> No Thought advances, but her Eddy Brain
> Whisks it about, and down it goes again.

22. Papillia's park is hardly a trifle, but she behaves as if it were and wants it thrown away.

23. *Enigmaticall Characters*, pp. 14-15.

small fortune and spends so much on vanities that she can rarely afford to be charitable. Yet if someone asks her for a donation to a charity when she "happens to be in a right temper, she will toss him half a crown or a crown, and tell him, if he knew what a long Milliner's bill she had just received, he would think it a great deal for her to give."[24] Pope's Narcissa

> paid a Tradesman once to make him stare;
> Gave alms at Easter, in a christian trim,
> And made a Widow happy, for a whim.

Two of Law's people should be noticed in connection with impatient, witty Flavia in the *Epistle to a Lady*. Flatus is rich and restless and perpetually striving. "His sanguine temper, and strong passions, promise him so much happiness in every thing, that he is always cheated, and satisfied with nothing."[25] Law's Caelia is similar in that though she is forever annoyed with people, she really "has nothing to torment her but her own spirit."[26] Pope's Flavia, a much more intricate person than either of these, resembles them none the less:

> With too much Spirit to be e'er at Ease,
> With too much Quickness ever to be taught,
> With too much Thinking to have common Thought:
> You purchase Pain with all that Joy can give,
> And die of nothing but a Rage to live.

---

24. P. 96. Pope quoted and ridiculed Law's *Absolute Unlawfulness of the Stage Entertainment* in the *Dunciad Variorum*. But Leslie Stephen argued that Pope's character-sketches resemble Law's and that one line in *To Bathurst*—"Meat, Fire, and Cloaths. What more? Meat, Cloaths, and Fire"—was suggested by Law's saying that "Meat, drink, and cloathing are the only things necessary in life." Cf. *History of English Thought in the Eighteenth Century* (1876), II, 399.

Another detail about Law's Flavia is worth noticing in connection with Pope's Silia, whose normal softness is transformed into storms and raving by "a Pimple on her nose." Law writes: "Flavia would be a miracle of Piety, if she was but half so careful of her soul, as she is of her body. The rising of a pimple in her face, the sting of a gnat, will make her keep her room two or three days" (p. 97). The use of this trivial annoyance in Young's first Satire is less relevant:

> This Passion [love of fame] with a pimple have I seen
> Retard a Cause, and give a Judge the spleen.

25. *A Serious Call*, p. 189.
26. *A Serious Call*, p. 170.

That one should come upon reminders of Pope in Law's *Serious Call* is not surprising. Even though Law would have rebelled at the thought of presenting in his earnestly religious book some of the vicious figures that Pope dealt with, he and Edward Young and Pope all worked their way across the country of the beau monde, to come inevitably upon some of the same kinds of people. Neither satiric poet could outdo the preacher in direct and honest speech as he views the rich, the leisurely, and the fashionable. Law's analysis, as Samuel Johnson learned, is undefeatable, and Pope if he read this book would surely have been impressed, whatever he thought of Law's other writings. Law and Young present a narrower range of social and moral types than Pope. But all three are confined to the gentry and aristocracy; their interests did not cause them to notice the country bumpkins, the actors, Oxford dons, hostlers, sailors, boys, or milkmaids that make Overbury's and John Stephens's and Earle's and Lenton's Character-books genuine microcosmographies. Flecknoe, one of the last authors to produce authentic Character-books, had frequented aristocratic society on the Continent, or so he said, and his experience of society seems to have led him to discoveries matching some of those of Law and Pope.

One might suppose that there were also precedents for some of Pope's figures in the bountiful supply of character-sketches in the *Tatler* and *Spectator*. Without doubt they could be found. Addison's joking about "Tulippomania" I have already mentioned. But like Law, Steele and Addison were not disposed to portray incorrigible or depraved creatures, types sometimes seen in Horace and Juvenal and Pope. What would be the use? Law patiently, remorselessly opens up the flaws in attitude and honesty and seriousness in "respectable" people; he hopes to save them by the simultaneous application of vivid description of their conduct and searching examination of their minds. Steele and Addison go a little farther into the open wickedness of society for an occasional subject. Yet the faults they rally are most often not frightful; by a shift in manners or a slight indulgence in common sense their sinners could become, if not saints, at least quite acceptable folk.

As will be suggested in Chapter VI, the large collection of worldly, vain, and discontented creatures that fills up Young's *Love of Fame the Universal Passion* offers many particular insights into the motives and standards of fashionable society that Pope's sketches also disclose. Like Law, Young anatomizes, though in infinitely briefer compass; but Young finds more really astonishing twists of mind to dramatize than do Law or Steele or Addison, and Pope undoubtedly profited from the material in his poems.[27]

What occurs to one in a comparison of Pope's and Young's sketches on one hand and those of Steele, Addison, and Law on the other is that the former writers are less interested than the latter in familiar types of character and that they are less willing to compose full, careful, strictly traditional drawings of them. When Pope chooses a well-recognized category—the miser, the false friend, the gourmet, the learned lady, the vain woman, the lecher, the *beatus ille,* the spendthrift—he tends either to treat it briefly (as in the sketches at the end of the *Epistle to Lord Cobham*) or to particularize it in some fashion (picturesque detail in "Artimesia," droll rationalization for Cotta's son, lavish pictorial presentation for Timon). The "Ode on Solitude" is unusual in its absolute traditionalism. In the four "Epistles to Several Persons" and the *Arbuthnot* Pope created figures so odd or so special that one is surprised to discover that some of them had precedents. Apparently Pope endeavored to brighten his poems with pictures of characters who would convey his messages to the world and yet, like the characters of Shakespeare, would seem each "as much an Individual, as those in Life itself."

His sketch of the good-natured critic in the *Essay on Criticism,* Steele's sketch of Aristaeus the genteel man (*Tatler* No. 176), and Addison's of Sombrius (*Spectator* No. 494) are about equally general. "About an Age ago," writes Addison,

---

27. Pope's general debt (rather than certain particular matters that I discuss here and in Chapter VI) is sketched in Charlotte E. Crawford's "What Was Pope's Debt to Edward Young?" in *ELH,* XIII (1946), 157-167. There are comparisons of Young, Pope, and La Bruyère also in W. Thomas's *Le Poète Edward Young* (Paris, 1901).

it was the Fashion in England, for every one that would be thought religious, to throw as much Sanctity as possible into his Face, and in particular
to abstain from all appearances of Mirth and Pleasantry, which were
looked upon as the Marks of a Carnal Mind. . . .

Sombrius is one of these Sons of Sorrow. He thinks himself obliged in
Duty to be sad and disconsolate. He looks on a sudden Fit of laughter, as
a Breach of his Baptismal Vow. An innocent Jest startles him like Blas-
phemy. Tell him of one who is advanced to a Title of Honour, he lifts up
his Hands and Eyes; describe a Publick Ceremony, he shakes his Head;
show him a gay Equipage, he blesses himself. All the little Ornaments of
Life are Pomps and Vanities. Mirth is wanton, and Wit prophane. He is
scandalized at Youth for being lively, and at Childhood for being playful.
He sits at a Christening, or a Marriage-Feast, as at a Funeral; sighs at
the Conclusion of a merry Story; and grows devout when the rest of the
Company grow pleasant. After all, Sombrius is a religious Man, and would
have behaved him self very properly, had he lived when Christianity was
under a general Persecution.

Pope's depiction of the good-natured critic we should meet in the
Tatler or *Spectator* with no sense of surprise, but the account of Sombrius is too predictable, too central, too Theophrastan in its data to
be Pope's work.

Encouragement to portray the eccentricities lurking behind the
façade of upper-class society came to Pope, as it came to Young, from
another collector of pictures of social and moral man, Jean de la
Bruyère, whose *Caractères* first appeared in 1688. La Bruyère's genius
for character-study was greater than that of any of the English writers
just mentioned, and the kind of stimulation he gave Pope was various.
Though Pope never copied La Bruyère as plainly as did Young (in
"Florio") and Eustace Budgell (in *Spectator* No. 77) nor acknowledged a debt publicly like Steele (in *Tatler* Nos. 9 and 57),[28] many
an idea from the French writer took root in Pope's imagination and
developed there into something new, though related.[29] I have already

---

28. The influence of La Bruyère on the *Tatler* and *Spectator* is pervasive. Some
aspects of the subject are treated in Edward C. Baldwin's "La Bruyère's Influence
upon Addison," *PMLA*, XIX (1904), 479-495, and in Margaret Turner's "The
Influence of La Bruyère on the 'Tatler' and the 'Spectator,' " *Modern Lang. Review*,
XLVIII (1953), 10-16.

29. Resemblances between passages in La Bruyère and in *To Burlington, To*

suggested precedents in the *Caractères* for Timon and the flower-fancier. What may at first seem invisible is a similarity in basic idea between La Bruyère's Character of Ruffin, the cheerful, unfeeling man, and Pope's Cloe.

"Cloe: A Character" was first printed in 1738 as a separate poem and appeared thus in three other printings before the lines were incorporated in the text of the *Epistle to a Lady* in the death-bed edition.[30] About thirty years after the death of Mrs. Howard (Lady Suffolk, Pope's good friend and King George's mistress), Joseph Warton suggested that she was the original for Cloe. But recently a cogent argument has been offered to show that if any details in the picture were derived from Mrs. Howard, the *tout ensemble* could not have been intended or taken as a portrait of her.[31] A comparison of Pope's figure and La Bruyère's may or may not suggest another possible source for Pope's picture, but it will help to clarify the quality of the latter.

Ruffinus begins to turn grey, but he's healthy; his Colour and quick Eye promise him at least twenty years more. He is gay, jolly, familiar, and

Cobham, To a Lady, Essay on Man, and *Dunciad IV* have been noticed in footnotes in Elwin-Courthope and the relevant volumes of the Twickenham Edition; also in Emile Audra, *L'Influence Française dans l'Oeuvre de Pope* (Paris, 1931), pp. 531-534, 555-560. In addition there are general resemblances between the *Caractères* and Pope's four *Epistles* in the subjects, in the loose grouping of material by theme, and in the distribution among *pensées* and epigrams of both long and short sketches, favorable and unfavorable.

I add a few more small, particular parallels. The Stoic wiseman, says La Bruyère in "De l'Homme," is unlike the foolish man who weeps and despairs "pour une porcelaine qui est en pieces." Similarly Pope praises the lady addressed in his *Epistle* for being "Mistress of yourself, tho' China fall." A coquette dies "parée et en rubans de couleur" ("Des Femmes"); compare Narcissa in *To Cobham.* A young abbé is very rich, and many whole families are very poor; "quel partage! Et cela ne prouve-t-il pas clairement un avenir?" (*Caractères,* I, 191). In *To Bathurst* after the account of Villiers's extravagance with money and miserly Cutler's indifference to the poor, Pope similarly exclaims:

>Say, for such worth are other worlds prepar'd?
>Or are they both, in this their own reward?

See pp. 62, 80, 87, 119-122 below for further material on the similarities between La Bruyère and Pope.

30. Ault and Butt, p. 377.

31. Norman Ault, *New Light on Pope* (1949), chap. xvi.

indifferent; he laughs heartily aloud, and fears nothing; he is content with himself and what belongs to him; he's satisfy'd with his little fortune, and calls himself happy. Some time since his only Son dy'd, who was the hopes of the Family, and might have been its honour; he resign'd his tears to others, he said, *My Son is dead, 'twill be the death of his Mother;* and was comforted. He has no passions, no friends nor enemies, no body troubles him, all the world agrees with him, every thing suits him, he talks to those he never saw before, with the same liberty and confidence as to those he calls his old friends; he tells them presently all his Stories and Puns. He is accosted, forsaken; he takes no notice on't, but the tale he begun to one person, he finishes to another that comes after him.[32]

Ruffin is a man. But Pope had already transformed Horace's Fufidienus into a woman. Ruffin and Cloe are outwardly pleasing examples of humanity, healthy and well set up; Ruffin has "un visage frais & un oeil vif," and Cloe "was form'd without a Spot," for Nature in her "err'd not." Both are indifferent to others (he is "indifferent," she "unmov'd"). Ruffin, having no passions, has neither friends nor enemies; Cloe has never loved nor been loved. Ruffin doesn't notice whether you come or go; Cloe bids her footman remind her if you are alive or dead. Ruffin's coldness shows especially in respect to parental love, Cloe's most strikingly in respect to carnal love, but their lack of feeling affects all their social contacts. Supplementing the main feature are corollaries: Ruffin's inability to respond emotionally to human occasions makes him singularly careless and inattentive when he is with people; Cloe's good breeding keeps her attentive to the decencies—except when she forgets.

But there is one puzzling feature in Pope's drawing: if Cloe never, never, had a generous thought and finds virtue too troublesome, why should she always keep your secret? Surely forgetfulness would as often expose her friends' confidences as obliterate them. The presence in the picture of this seeming incongruity gives it, indeed, the quality of reality, as if the author (or speaker, as he appears rather to be) were thinking about some particular incident in his relations with a

---

32. *The Characters, or the Manners of the Age. By Monsieur De La Bruyere . . . Made English by several hands . . . The Second Edition, Corrected throughout, and Enlarged* (1700), p. 240. The original from which this is closely translated appears in *Caractères,* I, 343-344.

particular person and were generalizing improperly from it. Pope's strongly reproachful attitude is another element that distinguishes his piece from La Bruyère's, in which the quiet curiosity of an invisible spectator stifles any expression of disapproval. Cloe is basically the amoral, self-indulgent lady of fashion that Pope frequently started with; her passionlessness defines her further, and the specific details, though startling, do not disturb the essence of a familiar type. But the reference to keeping secrets spoils the painting of a type and creates a unique, personally reported case. Ruffin, on the contrary, is an unfamiliar sort of fellow but entirely self-consistent. The dialogue-manner with which Pope opens his characterization, a device frequently adopted by La Bruyère though not for Ruffin, also contributes to the impression of personal acquaintance. Separate or in company the Cloe picture has an admirably double value—of representing someone, queer and interesting, who is very much an individual but who none the less dramatizes a common bad tendency in upper-class society. Ruffin is not so successful in this way.

Philomede in the *Epistle to a Lady* is another of Pope's astonishing figures whom annotators have wished to pin down as a portrait of a particular woman—Henrietta, the younger Duchess of Marlborough in this case. I can locate no exact model for her in the *Caractères,* but for the latter part of Pope's sketch (Philomede's lecturing all mankind on delicacy and taste in love and then heartily accepting a dunce for herself) it offers suggestions. La Bruyère reports that one lady he knew of, young, beautiful, disdainful, at last married not a hero as she led everyone to anticipate but a foolish little man ("un petit monstre qui manque d'esprit").[33] La Bruyère also said that ill-used lovers often have the revenge of seeing their mistresses throw themselves away on an old, ugly, or undeserving spouse.[34] Pope shifts from the lover's point of view of this last remark to that of disapproving, female society. Whether the *Caractères* or some particular woman or Pope's imagination working on various ancient themes in morality and manners should be chiefly credited

33. *Caractères,* I, 124.
34. *Caractères,* I, 135.

with the basic ideas for Cloe and Philomede no one can now say. But La Bruyère and Pope recorded some of the same oddities in human nature.

ii. Portraits of Actual Individuals

One would expect Pope's paintings of presumably imaginary figures to have points in common with earlier literary representations. Now let us consider certain of his indubitable portraits of historical individuals in the same retrospective way.

The earliest and most generally admired of these is his picture of Joseph Addison. Begun as early as 1715 and first published in *The St. James's Journal* for December 15, 1722, as a picture of "Ad——n," it underwent minor revisions in its several later reprintings before it finally was fitted into the *Epistle to Dr. Arbuthnot* in 1735. There it reads as follows:

> Peace to all such! but were there One whose fires
> True Genius kindles, and fair Fame inspires,
> Blest with each Talent and each Art to please,
> And born to write, converse, and live with ease:
> Shou'd such a man, too fond to rule alone,
> Bear, like the Turk, no brother near the throne,
> View him with scornful, yet with jealous eyes,
> And hate for Arts that caus'd himself to rise;
> Damn with faint praise, assent with civil leer,
> And without sneering, teach the rest to sneer;
> Willing to wound, and yet afraid to strike,
> Just hint a fault, and hesitate dislike;
> Alike reserv'd to blame, or to commend,
> A tim'rous foe, and a suspicious friend,
> Dreading ev'n fools, by Flatterers besieg'd,
> And so obliging that he ne'er oblig'd;
> Like Cato, give his little Senate laws,
> And sit attentive to his own applause;

> While Wits and Templers ev'ry sentence raise,
> And wonder with a foolish face of praise.
> Who but must laugh, if such a man there be?
> Who would not weep, if Atticus were he?

This is the man with whom, about 1715, Pope found it impossible to remain friendly. The Dean of Peterborough, who had many literary associations, said that "Atticus" fitted Addison truly,[35] and what one can learn about Addison nowadays does not destroy the plausibility of the portrait as far as it goes. But whether a fair representation of Addison or not, Atticus is imaginatively true; he embodies an artist's vision that is wholly persuasive.

Pope no doubt painted Addison as he saw him. But how did his imagination see him? As an "Eastern King" who destroyed all possible rivals—an image which Pope derived from *Spectator* Number 253, where it had been applied by Addison to Pope himself and to his treatment of others in the *Essay on Criticism*. Malone observed that Pope saw Addison in an ironic image taken from Wycherley's picture of writers who fear each other and "with faint Praises, one another Damn."[36] Pope's line, "Alike reserv'd to blame, or to commend," suggests that he also was measuring Addison in his mind by the standard of Walsh, whose portrait he had lightly sketched at the end of the *Essay on Criticism*—

> . . . . . . the Muse's judge and friend
> Who justly knew to blame or to commend.
> To failings mild, but zealous for desert;
> The clearest head, and the sincerest heart.

There is a longer passage that might have helped Pope "see" Atticus. When Addison's cousin Eustace Budgell published his translation of Theophrastus's *Characters* Pope was moved to write a set of scornful couplets about it that ridiculed Budgell for his barren mind and for the poor quality of his translation. Pope brought the little poem to an end as follows:

---

35. Spence, p. 57.
36. Prologue to *The Plain Dealer*. See Butt, p. 110 n.

But faith I fear, some Folks beside
These smart, new Characters supplyd.
The honest Fellow out at Heels
Pray between Friends, was not that Steel's?
The Rustic Lout so like a Brute,
Was Philips's beyond Dispute.
And the fond Fop so clean contrary,
Tis plain, tis very plain, was Cary.
Howe're, the Coxcomb's thy own Merit,
That thou hast done, with Life and Spirit.[37]

The thrust, by way of Theophrastus's Character of the Rustic, at the absurdly illiterate bumpkins in Ambrose Philips's pastorals is apt enough. But Budgell's volume contains no Character of a fellow out at heels, and only by some liberty of language or deletion of irrelevant sentences can one say that Theophrastus's collection presents the types of the fop (in "Vain-Glory"?) and the coxcomb (in "Impertinence in Discourse"? in "Ostentation"?). Pope was laughing at Addison's three friends by means of Theophrastan Characters of which one, if not all three, existed only in Pope's lively and inventive mind.

But a Character which Budgell's volume certainly did contain and which was placed at the beginning where Pope was bound to see it is that of a Dissembler, which opens thus:

Dissimulation is The Art of Speaking and Acting in Disguise, to bring about some Selfish Design. The Dissembler makes a Visit to his Enemy, as if he were so far from hating him that he took a particular Pleasure in his Conversation. He praises and caresses those whom he undermines, and is outwardly inconsolable for their Misfortunes, whilst he rejoices at them in his Heart. If you speak Ill of him, he is so Meek as to forgive you. If you utter the most bitter Invectives against him, he thanks you for telling him his Faults. After having done a Man an Injury he redoubles his Professions of Friendship, and sweetens him out of his Resentments . . . .

Pope probably encountered Budgell's Dissembler somewhere near the time when his friendship with a particular dissembler, Budgell's

---

37. Ault and Butt, p. 123.

cousin, was deteriorating so much that he felt moved to compose the famous lines about him; the *Characters* appeared in 1714 and the Atticus portrait was probably outlined late in 1715 or early in 1716.[38] If Pope "saw" Philips and three others of Addison's friends in Theophrastan Characters, why not Addison too? At least here was encouragement to define a particular case.[39]

Pope saw Addison as a subtle fusion of several types. First he recognizes the true genius, next the literary Turk, with whose type the jealous man[40] is then blended and the malicious dissembler and the timid man. Finally, as the tragi-comic result, he is the Cato of his carefully chosen senate, a good deal like La Bruyère's Arsène, "Loué, exalté, & porté jusqu'aux cieux par de certaines gens, qui se sont promis de s'admirer reciproquement" and superior to the commonplace duty of leading a life "suivie & uniforme."[41] In painting the portrait Pope worked from the life but in its composition took hints from Addison's allusion to "Eastern Kings," from the image of Cato in his own prologue to Addison's play, and perhaps from other literary sketches. In any acute portrait, as was remarked earlier, one may recognize intimations of other people, of classes of people, and Atticus is thus variously and permanently suggestive. But as Pope certainly intended, Atticus was, and always will be, Addison.

The flamboyant portrait of Clodio (Philip, Duke of Wharton) in the *Epistle to Lord Cobham* attempts to present a more varied personality than Addison's, and the levy upon art is more conspicuous and less successful.

---

38. Ault, *New Light on Pope*, p. 124.

39. What the Theophrastan Character of Dissimulation resembles more closely than Atticus is the whole story, as Pope gave it out, of his quarrel with Addison, including the account in Spence (pp. 148-149) of how Pope threatened him with this very "Invective," the Atticus lines, and how Addison became "Meek" and inoffensive thereafter. But unless we are to assume that Pope's version of the whole affair was partly invented, there can be no causal connection between "Dissimulation" and Spence's narrative. Yet the similarities are amusing.

40. See *Notes and Queries*, N.S. VIII (July, 1961), 253, for John Crossett's argument that Pope drew on Joseph Hall's Character of the Envious Man for ll. 7-12.

41. *Caractères*, I, 82-83. For an outline of the type of "fearful" man to which Atticus might be said to belong see La Chambre's description given below, n. 59.

Clodio, the Scorn and Wonder of our days,
Whose ruling passion was the Lust of Praise;
Born with whate'er could win it from the wise,
Women and Fools must like him, or he dies.
Tho' wond'ring Senates hung on all he spoke,
The club must hail him Master of the Joke.
Shall parts so various aim at nothing new?
He'll shine a Tully, and a Wilmot too:
Then turns repentant, and his God adores
With the same Spirit that he drinks and whores:
Enough, if all around him but admire,
And now the Punk applaud, and now the Fry'r.
Thus, with each gift of Nature and of Art,
And wanting nothing but an honest heart;
Grown all to all, from no one Vice exempt,
And most contemptible to shun Contempt;
His Passion still to covet gen'ral praise,
His Life, to forfeit it a thousand ways;
His constant Bounty no one friend has made;
His Angel Tongue no mortal can persuade:
A Fool, with more of Wit than half mankind,
Too rash for Thought, for Action too refin'd:
A Tyrant to the Wife his heart approves;
A Rebel to the very King he loves;
He dies, sad out-cast of each Church and State!
And (harder still) flagitious, yet not great!
Ask you why Clodio broke thro' every rule?
'Twas all for fear, the Knaves shou'd call him Fool.[42]

Pope had some sort of personal acquaintance with Wharton, but it is not evident that the two were ever intimate. Ten years younger than Pope, Wharton was the son of Addison's patron. Lady Mary Wortley Montagu's father was one of his guardians under the elder

---

42. *An Epistle to the Right Honourable Richard Lord Visc^t. Cobham* (1733), pp. 9-11.

Wharton's will, and, perhaps to be near him, Wharton took a house at Twickenham in 1722.[43] Lady Mary declared that the young nobleman's attentions to her annoyed Pope, but her friendship with the mercurial Wharton and their alleged collaboration in writing squibs did not last long. The remark jotted down by Edward Harley in the late 1720's that Wharton "had extream good parts" but was "not to be imitated"[44] agrees with the extended portrayal in the anonymous *Memoirs of the Life of his Grace Philip late Duke of Wharton* (1731). In that sober work, which emphasizes Wharton's remarkable charm, wit, and quick apprehension in order to counterpoise the revelation of his inborn inconstancy and wildness, he is presented as "the merriest undone Man in Europe" (p. 32), shameless in his escapades, thoughtless of the morrow, a victim of every impulse.

Pope's portrait, remarkably compendious in respect to the facts of Wharton's career, offers an interpretation of the facts only partly adumbrated in the *Memoirs*. The kernel of the interpretation—that Wharton was driven by "the Lust of Praise"—no doubt came to Pope's mind easily. He had twice before written of how literary men might be forced into unworthy behavior by their "lust of praise" (called "sacred" in the *Essay on Criticism*, but "wretched" in the *Temple of Fame*). This last infirmity of noble minds was something which interested Pope—for whatever reason.[45] But I think he may have been encouraged to adopt so glib an explanation of Philip Wharton's strange course partly because of the ironic contrast it would present with the estimate often given of his father, Thomas, Earl of Wharton. Swift, in his excoriating *Short Character of His Ex. T. E. of W.* (1711), declared that the Earl was ruled by "three predominant Passions, which you will seldom find united in the same Man . . . Love of Power, Love of Money, and Love of Pleasure." Wharton was, Swift says, "indifferent . . . to Applause, and . . . insensible of Reproach." Swift's colleague Mrs. Manley in her long

43. Robert Halsband, *The Life of Lady Mary Wortley Montagu* (Oxford, 1956), p. 113.

44. British Museum MS Loan 29/ 338, p. 54.

45. I am indebted to Aubrey L. Williams for calling my attention to Pope's several references to "lust of praise" and "lust of fame."

and equally harsh description of the elder Wharton[46] likewise presents him as shameless; he has only "this one Virtue, *not pretending
to any.*" This feature of being indifferent to fame Pope turns upside
down in the son,

> Whose ruling passion was the Lust of Praise;
>
> .   .   .   .
>
> His Passion still to covet gen'ral praise,
>
> .   .   .   .
>
> Ask you why Clodio broke thro' every rule?
> 'Twas all for fear, the Knaves shou'd call him Fool.

Mrs. Manley finds in the father the extremes of conduct that
Pope assigns to the son. Wharton would sin, she writes,

up to the Height of Pleasure, yet drudge on to the last Extremity of Business: Indefatigable in his Pursuits; not by Fits and Starts, but by a regular
Succession: Vast was his Ambition, vast was his Artifice . . . No View of
his, tho' never so trivial, but what he bent his whole Endeavours to obtain,
and always accomplish'd. . . . He would play with the Gamester, pray with
the Godly, be lewd with the Libertine, and, rather than fail, pimp for
him, tho' his own Wife were the Mistress; he was drunk with the De-
bauchee, sober with the Abstemious . . . .

We seem to be encountering the same conduct, though not the same
motive, in Pope's account of the son, who

> . . . turns repentant, and his God adores
> With the same Spirit that he drinks and whores:
> Enough, if all around him but admire,
> And now the Punk applaud, and now the Fry'r.

Pope read three passages about the elder Wharton in his copy
of *A New Collection of Poems Relating to State Affairs,* jotting
down Wharton's name beside each. In "The Golden Age Revers'd"
by Pope's old friend, "knowing Walsh," the attack is heavily ironic:
the Whig politician is said to be famous for valor, truth, justice, and
freedom from faction. In "Faction Display'd" by another of Pope's

---

46. *Secret Memoirs, . . . from the New Atalantis* (1720), III, 189-191.

good men ("downright Shippen"), Clodio, as the elder Wharton is here called, is portrayed with features attributed by Pope to his son (whom Pope calls Clodio):

> Clodio, the Chief of all the Rebel-Race,
> Uncheck'd by Fear, unhumbled by Disgrace;
> Whose Working, Turbulent, Fanatick, Mind
> No Tenderness can move, no Ties can bind.
> To gain a Rake, he'll Drink, and Whore, and Rant,
> T'engage a Puritan, will Pray and Cant.[47]

The fourth of these lines could be imagined to have been transformed into Pope's couplet,

> A Tyrant to the Wife his heart approves;
> A Rebel to the very King he loves.

Philip Wharton's sudden (but temporary) public doting on his wife in 1724 seems to have impressed Pope more favorably than it did Lady Mary,[48] and Pope gives him the benefit of any doubts. As for the king he loved, since Wharton turned traitor to George, then to the Pretender, then to George again, one might wonder which royal person Pope had in mind when he composed the especially dubious half of the quadrilateral rhetoric of the couplet. The Rake-Puritan extremes in Shippen's account of the father reappear in Pope's Punk-Fry'r opposition. Shippen provided a sample of the oratory of the father; but the oratory of the son, which was well known and in print, Pope only mentions.

There is something odd about Pope's appropriating the name Clodio, originally given to Thomas Wharton, for his son. Surely Pope was acquainted with Philip Wharton's periodical, *The True Briton,* with its prolonged defense of Pope's friend, Bishop Atterbury, and he may have seen Number 43 (Oct. 28, 1723). In that issue appears a pindaric ode which laments the exile from Rome of Cicero

---

47. *A New Collection of Poems Relating to State Affairs* (1705), p. 575.
48. *The Letters and Works of Lady Mary Wortley Montagu,* ed. Lord Wharncliffe and W. Moy Thomas (1893), I, 478.

(Atterbury) and condemns the "lewd Roman Senator" Clodius (Walpole) for the plots, perjuries, and bribes that brought about that exile. The poem alarmingly announces that after a short reign Clodius will be stabbed and will ingloriously die. The Jacobite Shippen had applied the label "Clodio" to the powerful Whig Thomas Wharton; Wharton's son, now seemingly Jacobite in sympathy, used the epithet for another great Whig, Walpole. But Pope's adoption of the name for the whirligig son was probably not for its political coloration but because of its having become a family possession, so to speak.

The True Briton, ranging from the murderous encouragements of Number 43 to the sanctimonious piety of the Character of "a Christian Politician" in Number 54, satisfies one's expectations of inconsistency in its author. Likewise it indicates in Wharton a capacity for at least lip-service to virtue and honesty (especially in the Character of "The Honest Man" in Number 58). The *Memoirs* insisted that people were wrong to say that Wharton had lacked honor and principle. Pope entered several merits into the mixture of Wharton's character as he portrayed it, but he ruined all and contradicted the *Memoirs* by denying him "an honest heart." Thus he could make of Wharton what he needed for his poem, an image of the most inconsistent of men.

Pope may have been seduced into this perpetually contradictory design of character by Dryden's similarly benign-caustic portrait of Buckingham ("Zimri") as much as by the *Memoirs* or whatever else he knew about the man. Also he was composing the sketch to illustrate a theory. He wished to prove that the most puzzling character can be understood if his ruling passion is discovered, and to demonstrate the unity in Wharton Pope took for his key the reverse of what was said to be the elder Wharton's nature. That the desire to be praised by everyone, including fools and knaves, might cause a man to lose the respect of wife, king, and friends is likely enough. But "to shun Contempt" is not quite the same as "to covet gen'ral praise," though Pope indulges in this forced identity a second time in order to bring the sketch to a resounding finale in the word "Fool." And neither in the details here assembled nor in the recorded facts of his life does

Wharton appear to be "Too rash for Thought, for Action too refin'd." Pope's search for inconsistencies "carries him far beyond his theory."[49] The force of the picture is not in the paradoxical key, the ruling passion, but in the extravagant, all-inclusive, jarring self-contradictions. Like La Bruyère's picture of the absent-minded man Ménalque[50] with its incredibly long list of laughable instances, Pope's sketch is delightful to read but fails to create an image of a really credible individual. Without the glitter of its rhetoric and poetics the picture would show its weakness at once.

In the case of the well-known account of John Kyrle, the Man of Ross, in the *Epistle to Lord Bathurst* Pope was not personally acquainted with his subject and obtained much of his material from the younger Jacob Tonson, confessing to a "small exaggeration" in the representation. Warburton noted that one of the exaggerations was the incorrect implication that Kyrle's philanthropies had been possible on an income of so little as five hundred pounds a year. In Law's *Serious Call* Pope could have found a whole chapter (VIII) on the "wise and pious Use of an Estate" illustrated at length by an account of Miranda, sister of the selfish, uncharitable Flavia whom I have mentioned in connection with Pope's Narcissa. Miranda is as different from her sister as the Man of Ross from George Villiers with whom he is contrasted. She sets up people in business, she educates foundlings, she helps the poor and aged, and all on an income of two hundred pounds a year. Law tells a good deal about her, including her religious code, her ways of thinking, her daily behavior. He knows her well, at least in his imagination. But Pope characterizes Kyrle only by the implications of a list of his good deeds, some of which duplicate Miranda's. Biblical echoes[51] help to keep the picture dispersed and prevent it from "composing." Consequently, though an historical person, the Man of Ross does not appear as a directly encountered individual. What we have is not so much a character-

---

49. Reuben A. Brower, *Alexander Pope* (Oxford, 1959), p. 264.
50. In the chapter "De l'Homme."
51. See Earl R. Wasserman, *Pope's Epistle to Bathurst: A Critical Reading* (Baltimore, 1960), pp. 41-42.

sketch as a scenic biography, like Law's chapter in its homiletic purpose but lacking Law's customary subjective interest.

Pope told Spence that he had omitted, presumably from the
Essay on Man, "a character (though I thought it one of the best I
had ever written) of a very great man who had every thing from
without to make him happy, and yet was very miserable; from the
want of virtue in his own heart."[52] Spence supposed the unnamed
man was the Duke of Marlborough, and we may safely agree. The
following lines, written in Pope's hand on a leaf from a copy of the
1734 quarto edition of the *Essay,* must be those alluded to.

> Mark by what wretched steps Great ** grows,
> From dirt and sea-weed as proud Venice rose;
> One equal course how Guilt and Greatness ran,
> And all that rais'd the Hero sunk the Man.
> Now Europe's Lawrels on his brows behold,
> But stain'd with Blood, or ill exchang'd for Gold:
> What wonder tryumphs never turn'd his brain
> Fill'd with mean fear to lose mean joy to gain.
> Hence see him modest free from pride or shew
> Some Vices were too high but none too low
> Go then indulge thy age in Wealth & ease
> Stretch'd on the spoils of plunder'd palaces
> Alas what wealth, which no one act of fame
> E'er taught to shine, or sanctified from shame
> Alas what ease those furies of thy life
> Ambition Av'rice & th' imperious Wife
> The trophy'd Arches, story'd Halls invade,
> And haunt their slumbers in the pompous Shade.
> No joy no pleasure from successes past
> Timid & therefore treacherous to the last
> Hear him in accents of a pining Ghost
> Sigh, with his Captive for his ofspring lost

52. *Anecdotes,* p. 143.

> Behold him loaded with irreverend years
> Bath'd in unmeaning unrepentant tears
> Dead, by regardless Vet'rans born on high
> Dry pomps & Obsequies without a sigh.[53]

Because of the vocal style of the speaker there is some awkwardness for the reader in the grammatical shifts between second and third person and in the movement of thought between past and imaginary present. But the effect is splendid. If we are to consider the passage as a "character"—and Spence indicates that we should—we may sense some gaps if not mysteries beyond the open paradoxes. "Great **" is a man of low origins and high military triumphs, great but guilty and unrepentant; of mean vices but without certain loftier ones;[54] rich in gold but unable to enjoy it; a bloody conqueror but driven by an imperious wife—these are the public contradictions, and one can readily imagine them. But if modest and free from show, why his "fury" of ambition? If timid to the last, how so great a hero? The steady man whose triumphs never turned his brain—how the victim of three "furies"? All of these questions can be answered, though not always as Pope might wish them to be, in contemporary accounts of Marlborough. If he had somehow worked into the passage the interpretation of the Duke that he gave to Spence, the portrait would have been clearer, if not also truer, on one point—how a "fury" may make one calm and clear-headed. "Inconsistent as the Duke of Marlborough's character may appear to you," said Pope, "yet, may it be accounted for, if you gauge his actions by his reigning passion, which

---

53. Reproduced, with permission, from the original in the Yale University Library. I have modified the punctuation slightly, deleting a period after "Wife" which belonged only, I think, in a previous, crossed-out version of this part of the passage. In "And haunt their slumbers" "thy" should have been substituted for "their," but Pope neglected that change. I have omitted at the end twelve lines which would have fitted the portrait into the thought of the *Essay*. They dwell on the ignominious and shameful sequence of events in the Churchill family after the Duke's death. They make the portrait more plainly an epitaph but do not contribute to the characterization.

54. La Bruyère's "Aemile" (*Caractères*, I, 112-114), a highly laudatory portrait of the great Condé, La Bruyère's employer, mentions several of his military capabilities and concludes: "il n'a manqué que les moindres vertus."

was the love of money . . . . He was calm in the heat of battle; and when he was so near being taken prisoner (in his first campaign) in Flanders, he was quite unmoved . . . there was none of his money at stake . . . ."[55]

Contemporary writers often speak of Marlborough's unusual climb—from the dunghill, said the *Entertainer* (Number 27),[56] to "the character of a Prince," said the *Tatler* (Number 5). All but his most devoted partisans mention his avarice; even Burnet, who regarded the Duke as "one of the greatest men the age has produced,"[57] speaks of his habitual effort to acquire money and his parsimony in spending it. The Dutch officer, Sicco Van Goslinga, whose pen-portrait of his commander is accepted by Sir Winston Churchill as reliable, writes of the Duke's "avarice sordide . . . qui influe dans toute sa conduite."[58] Mrs. Manley makes avarice a key to Marlborough's character.

Timid to the last? Goslinga says there can be no doubt about the Duke's courage, though sometimes on the eve of battle he is irresolute and unsteady. Mrs. Manley, with a dramatic touch like Sallust's in revealing Catiline, tells us that "His Flatterers cry up his Courage, but it seems to me not to be so much inborn to him, as acquir'd . . . . A Proof . . . may be taken from always ducking his Head at the Noise of a Bullet; the first Apprehension is in his Nature, and only to be controul'd, not prevented, by Reason, which . . . carries him safely through to Glory."[59] There is much in Mrs. Manley's long analytical

---

55. Spence, p. 162.

56. Perhaps Pope had heard from Edward Harley that Marlborough's great-grandfather was "a Blacksmith whose shop was at Bradford by Dorchester" (British Museum MS Loan 29/349, fol. 8v). Sir Winston Churchill neither accepts nor rejects this rarely-mentioned allegation; see *Marlborough: His Life and Times*, I (1933), 30.

57. *History of His Own Time*, I (1724), 765. According to Courthope (Elwin-Courthope, II, 449 n.), Pope took from Burnet's saying of Marlborough "that he was in no contrivance to ruin or betray" James II the idea for his line in the *Essay on Man*, just where the portrait of Marlborough would have been inserted, "How happy! those to ruin, these betray."

58. *Memoires*, ed. U. A. Evertzz and G. H. M. Delprat (Leeuwarden, 1857), p. 43.

59. *Secret Memoirs*, I, 37. Mrs. Manley's alluding to Marlborough's drawing "the Spoils of Cities, of Provinces, of whole Nations" into his coffers (III, 28) is

account of the Duke to suggest Pope's, not least her somewhat unexpected way of standing off from her subject as he does, to see the
waste in the spectacle, the limitations that kept Marlborough from
true greatness. Her remarks come to an end in a query as to how he
will "descend to his Grave," whether after some sort of "Royal Cast,
an Imperial Squander," or just in "a most prodigious, accumulated
Mass of Wealth." Pope's image of the Duke buried and haunted "in
the pompous Shade" answers her question.

What Pope omits which Goslinga and Burnet and Mrs. Manley
and others include would be important if the aim of this passage were
true portraiture—the Duke's handsome face and irresistibly graceful
manner, his astuteness and "exact prudence" (Steele's phrase) and
depth of insight and "Length of View" (Mrs. Manley's), supported
by moderation and a perfectly governed temper, which last characteristic is not necessarily implied by Pope's word "modest." All
these traits are needed to explain Marlborough's rise. But Pope as
moralist is commenting on his fall. The portrait has the marmoreal
quality of an epitaph. It is a bitter epitaph, sharing the point of view
of Swift's attack in the *Examiner*. It is a corrective to Addison's
extravagant praise of the victorious general in *The Campaign*, where
Pope's phrase "the Hero and the Man" had been part of one laudatory passage and Pope's verb "shine" had been used for Marlborough's
"genius" and also for his great exploits.[60] Had the lines been pub-

---

to be noticed beside Pope's reference to "the spoils of plunder'd palaces" (a revision of the line "Or infamous for plunder'd Provinces" in the printed poem).

  That the character of Marlborough as Pope presents it is too complex to seem
typical can be shown by reference to what one of the treatises on the passions had
to say about the "fearful" man as a type: "when we know a man is fearful, we may
assure our selves that he is inclined to Avarice, that he is cunning and dissembling,
that he usually speaks softly and submissively, that he is suspicious, incredulous, an
ill friend, and the like" (*The Characters Of the Passions . . . by the Sieur de la
Chambre . . . Translated into English* [1659], "A Necessary Advertisement to the
Reader"). Marlborough, Pope indicates, is in addition furiously ambitious and a
bloody, victorious commander.

  60. The possibility that there was some connection between this scornful epitaph
and Creti's painting of Marlborough's tomb, one of a set of Italian paintings done
in the 1720's and 1730's in honor of prominent Whigs, is suggested in an article of
mine to appear in 1961 in *Criticism*, entitled "Baroque into Satire: Pope's Frontispiece for the *Essay on Man*."

lished in the *Essay on Man* they would have diverted the poem from "philosophy" to politics and satire, and Pope did well to leave them out.

Neither Marlborough nor Wharton was one of Pope's intimates. The bright movement of antithesis and the perpetual stimulation of paradox make the Wharton portrait memorable, and the appropriate grandeur of the imagery and intense bitterness of feeling give the Marlborough great force. A little help from previously published writing seems to have gone into both pictures. Joseph Addison was hardly the sort to open himself up to people freely, but Pope undoubtedly knew him more intimately than he did Wharton, and the portrait he made of him is the most subjective and detailed and imaginatively persuasive of all his sketches of identifiable people. Yet we have seen that he composed it also in part by the natural method of summoning up images of types of character and of behavior recorded in earlier publications. Bolingbroke, William Walsh, and John Gay are three others of Pope's acquaintance whom he sketched and for whose portraits he found it desirable to make use of more or less familiar patterns of human nature.

The brief, eulogistic sketch of Bolingbroke that Pope placed at the end of the *Essay on Man* serves its purpose very well.

> Teach me like thee, in various Nature wise,
> To fall with Dignity, with Temper rise;
> Form'd by thy Converse, happily to steer
> From grave to gay, from lively to severe,
> Correct with spirit, eloquent with ease,
> Intent to reason, or polite to please.

Reminding the reader of the salutation to Bolingbroke at the beginning of the *Essay* and of the proposal that they should together attempt to "vindicate the Ways of God to Man," the lines lead to another expression of respect for their friendship and to a brief summary of the "philosophy" Pope had found and explained. The six-line characterization of Bolingbroke's mind and manners may have been as true to the facts as Pope could possibly make them. But, as commentators have shown,[61] the four last lines are a composite of phrases from Quintilian's characterization of Homer, Horace's and Boileau's of the universally admirable writer, and Mallet's of Horace.

Somewhat similarly, the four-line picture of Walsh offered almost at the end of the *Essay on Criticism* seems to be a personal portrait and yet to have been adapted from another writer's representation of a different subject—Horace's account almost at the conclusion of the *Ars Poetica* of Quintilius Varus, his friendly critic. Pope's line, "The clearest Head, and the sincerest Heart," is a modernization of Horace's "vir bonus et prudens," a phrase used to name the type of which Varus was a much-cherished particular example.

These sketches of Bolingbroke and Walsh, because of the brevity necessitated by their function in the poems, could not provide much detail about individual temperament and behavior. In both cases the literary echoes—if the reader can catch them—are really needed to help express the praise intended; similarities between the ancient portraits and the modern were expected to be appreciated. Pope's epitaph on John Gay is also a laudatory piece, though the outlines of its subject are drawn more exactly and reveal, at least to the knowing, a hint of Gay's most serious flaw. Once more Pope requires the reader to imagine the person portrayed by calling to mind certain recognizable human patterns—

> In Wit, a Man; Simplicity, a Child;
>
> .   .   .   .
>
> A safe Companion, and an easy Friend.

For a public epitaph, very familiar images rather than delicate analysis are appropriate.

In many more of Pope's portraits—of his father in the *Epistle to Dr. Arbuthnot*, of George Villiers in the *Epistle to Lord Bathurst*, of Bentley in the *Dunciad* Book IV—one is led to have recollections of other people or intimations of classes of men. Pope's very graceful and suddenly serious way of depicting Lord Cobham as the true patriot in the finale of the *Epistle* addressed to him also illustrates

---

61. Mack, p. 165.

how well he could take advantage of the portrait-painter's opportunity to abstract, to exaggerate, to normalize the individual. The famous picture of Sporus, built up with damning phrases partly culled from previous pictures of Lord Hervey, is a different kind of example; for the man who fought a duel and begot eight children could not have been precisely and merely the creature Pope presented as Sporus. In order to create a shocking image of a special sort of vice Pope selected only certain aspects of a man who must have been in reality still more complex and curious than in the poem he seems. One is tempted to propose the neat generalization that in Pope's depictions the type tends to become more individual and the individual more typical. In the large I believe this is true. But there are exceptions. The portrait of Marlborough, for example, though grandly general in phrasing and though incomplete and even puzzling in its portrayal, seems to fit only the one extraordinary person. The portrait of Trumbull distinguishes its subject from the "happy man" of numerous earlier depictions by the addition of specific details about Trumbull's personal life. Yet even this picture, partly because of the Vergilian tone of admiration and partly because of the allusions at the end to Scipio and Atticus, is widely evocative. Actually Pope has left us no pen-portrait of any known person that could properly be judged absolutely faithful, unbiased, and complete. Recollecting the liveliness and the penetrating observation of some of his sketches, one might for a moment regret this lack; one might wish that in place of the paintings of Swift that he threw away Pope had recorded in unforgettable words his full knowledge of his friend. But the wish is foolish. Pope was a great poet and a superb satirist; the great historian is something different.

CHAPTER V

METHOD *and* TECHNIQUE

IT would be difficult to say how many ways there are for depicting in a continuous, circumscribed sketch either an actual figure or an imaginary one. But certain methods fell under Pope's eye, and we may suppose he noticed them. In the present chapter we shall consider the craft of the portrait-painter-in-verse.

The most formal sort of character-sketch Pope attempted only in a limited way. That is the stylized technique for portraying types of men which was admirably developed by Theophrastus and successfully imitated and extended by Joseph Hall, Sir Thomas Overbury, John Earle, and many more. Perhaps Pope thought the Character old-fashioned and mechanical; perhaps he associated Theophrastus with his translator Budgell (though there were two other English translations published during the first quarter of the century). But more important, the Character has a strictness of form which when combined with the additional regularity of meter had often produced something lifeless. The Character is a prose form. Its method originally was to begin with a definition and usually the formula "He is the sort of man who . . . ." It was composed in the present tense, the material accumulating in a series of situations in which by his customary actions and words the man reveals the essence of himself and his class. In the Characters of Theophrastus the subject does not appear to have been posed by a skilful artist; he is just a "Man Uninstructed, Unobserving, Unreflecting."[1]

The closest Pope came to creating a Character is the passage first published separately in the *London Evening Post* (January 22-25,

---

1. *Proposals for Printing by Subscription, 4000 Copies of the Characters of Theophrastus . . . By R. Newton* (Oxford, 1752), p. [v].

1732) and then incorporated, as follows, in the *Epistle to Dr. Arbuthnot:*

> The Fop whose pride affects a Patron's name,
> Yet absent, wounds an Author's honest fame;
> Who can your Merit selfishly approve,
> And show the Sense of it, without the Love;
> Who has the Vanity to call you Friend,
> Yet wants the Honour injur'd to defend;
> Who tells whate'er you think, whate'er you say,
> And, if he lyes not, must at least betray:
> Who to the Dean and silver Bell can swear,
> And sees at Cannons what was never there:
> Who reads but with a Lust to mis-apply,
> Make Satire a Lampoon, and Fiction, Lye.
> A Lash like mine no honest man shall dread,
> But all such babling blockheads in his stead.

The details here, except for the local references in lines nine and ten, are universally representative and hence Theophrastan. The organization too is Theophrastan: "The Fop whose pride . . . , Who can . . . , Who has . . . , Who tells . . . , Who to the Dean . . . , Who reads . . . ." Like the majority of seventeenth-century Characters this sketch combines objective revelation with subjective analysis. Pope owed the form of this presentation as well as the core of his subject to a five-line sketch of a back-biter in Horace.[2] In the Latin there were five *qui*-clauses; in Pope's first-published version of these lines there were five *who*- and *whose*-clauses, and here there are six. Pope's changes for his final version (a shift in lines five and seven from "me" and "I" to "you," and the adding of one more *who*-clause) increase the Character-like appearance of the sketch.

Similar in syntactical organization is the brief characterization of the good country gentleman in the *Epistle to Lord Burlington* (ll. 181-190). Although the depiction catches the more permanent features of its subject, it depends upon place and scene more than

2. *Sat.*, I, iv, 81-85.

Theophrastus ever did. Neither of the sketches is as classical and beautifully illustrative of a type of character as, for example, many of Richard Flecknoe's or Richard Steele's contributions to the genre. The pictures of Bufo in the *Epistle to Dr. Arbuthnot* and of Peter Waters in the imitation of Donne's second Satire (ll. 65-78) are rather like Characters in the method of assembling details of customary behavior in order to reveal the nature of the man. But the details are *in toto* so unusual that both passages seem to be personal portraits.

The formal scheme of the analytical, subjective Character popularized by Joseph Hall is suggested in Pope's early sketch of the good critic (really the good man who is also a critic):

> But where's the Man, who Counsel can bestow,
> Still pleas'd to teach, and yet not proud to know?
> Unbias'd, or by Favour or by Spite;
> Not dully prepossest, or blindly right;
> Tho' Learn'd, well-bred; and tho' well-bred, sincere;
> Modestly bold, and Humanly severe?
> Who to a Friend his Faults can freely show,
> And gladly praise the Merit of a Foe?
> Blest with a Taste exact, yet unconfin'd;
> A Knowledge both of Books and Humankind;
> Gen'rous Converse; a Soul exempt from Pride;
> And Love to Praise, with Reason on his Side?
>
> (*Essay on Criticism* [1711], pp. 36-37)

Probably inspired by Horace's account (similarly placed near the end of his *Ars Poetica*) of how Quintilius Varus and a "vir bonus et prudens" would criticize a poet's work, Pope's picture is more formal and also more inclusive.[3] The presentation is much too compressed for Hall; it depends too heavily in the first six lines upon adjectives and too little upon illustrative circumstances. Yet in spirit, in intention, in strict generality it duplicates important features of Hall's Characters of virtuous types.

---

3. See above p. 74 on Pope's use of Horace's material for the portrait of Walsh.

There is in the *Dunciad* (IV, 459-492 [Sutherland]) a modified version of the "credo-Character," the sort of sketch that aims to present chiefly the doctrine or point of view of a separate group of men rather than their whole personality. The essential feature of the figure portrayed in such pieces is intellectual. Hundreds of Characters of this sort poured from the presses during the troubled 1640's and 1650's in attack and in defense. Swift's "Sentiments of a Church-of-England Man" may be regarded as a late addition to that pamphleteering flow. The credo-Characters had tended to get out of hand; zeal, anger, a desire to destroy many offenders with one blow caused the literary form to disintegrate sometimes almost beyond recognition. Pope's representation of the mechanistic-rationalistic philosopher suffers from the last-named tendency; his "gloomy Clerk" states what "we" believe and "we" reject, but since "we" (the group the Clerk represents) are said, in the text and in the footnotes, to include Lucretius, Hobbes, Descartes, Spinoza, Tindal, some late Platonists, and Silenus too, the speaker's voice is hard to recognize, his identity difficult to specify.[4] As was true of some of the polemic Characters of Schismatics, Formalists, Sectaries, Levellers, and other groups in the middle seventeenth century, the target here is so multifarious that the sketch could interest only by its witticisms, not by accuracy; and Pope in these lines is not very witty.[5]

The satires of Horace, Juvenal, and Boileau gain much of their liveliness from numerous hasty but vivid glimpses of types of human folly and vice. These passages are sometimes like miniature or fragmentary Characters. Horace's miser (*Sat.*, II, ii, 55-62), his backbiter (I, iv, 81-85, the original for the fop-patron in the *Epistle to Dr. Arbuthnot*), and the more amply suggested legacy-hunter (II, v, 23-50) and parasite (*Epist.*, I, xv, 26-41) are objectively and graphi-

4. According to Arthur Friedman ("Pope and Deism," in *Pope and His Contemporaries: Essays Presented to George Sherburn*, ed. Jas. L. Clifford and Louis A. Landa [Oxford, 1949], pp. 89-95), Pope's contemporaries would have recognized that he was attacking the deist Toland. The speaker, nevertheless, is not clearly outlined.

5. The presentation earlier in Book IV of Aristarchus might also at first seem like a credo-Character. Yet it is less the pedant's doctrine than the lamentable results of the doctrine in action that Pope specifies.

cally presented in the way that Pope presented Bufo, old Cotta, and the set of eight types at the end of the *Epistle to Lord Cobham*. But Pope is more likely than Horace or Boileau or even Juvenal to arrange his material for the effect of wit and surprise. Probably in this respect he was encouraged by the example of La Bruyère, one of whose several kinds of *pensées* is an adaptation of the brief Roman sketch to give it the sting of the epigram.[6] Thus La Bruyère writes: "L'on ne se rend point sur le desir de posseder & de s'agrandir; la bile gagne, & la mort approche, qu'avec un visage flétri, & des jambes déja foibles l'on dit, *ma fortune, mon établissement*."[7] Pope's slightly expanded picture of the same truth in the *Epistle to Lord Cobham* illustrates not only his technical virtuosity in the couplet but also his capacity for revealing character dramatically:

> "I give and I devise (old Euclio said,
> And sigh'd) "my Lands and Tenements to Ned."
> Your Money Sir? "My Money Sir! what all?
> "Why —— if I must —— (then wept) I give it Paul."
> The Mannor, Sir?—"The Mannor! hold, he cry'd,
> "Not that —— I cannot part with that" —— and dy'd.

Some of Pope's sketches make one think of the shallow but pungent lampoons of Restoration days. His "Artimesia"[8] he indicated was in imitation of Dorset's manner; it includes Dorset's habitual simplification of his subject and his employment of an insect or animal simile (here it is a magpie) to increase the hatefulness of the victim. Pope kept the pejorative insect image in his repertoire not only for "Phryne" ("Grubs obscene" and worms and butterflies), which is another imitation of Dorset published in *Miscellanies*, but also for

6. La Bruyère's methods for developing sketches are too numerous to mention, and they often duplicate methods employed by Theophrastus, Horace, Juvenal, Martial, and the English Character-writers. For discussion of his methods see Paul Morillot, *La Bruyère* (Paris, 1904), pp. 116-117; the footnotes in Gaston Cayrou's edition (Paris, 1926); Pierre Richard, *La Bruyère et ses Caractères* (Amiens, 1946); Margaret Turner, "The Influence of La Bruyère on the 'Tatler' and the 'Spectator,'" *Mod. Lang. Review*, XLVIII (1953), 10-16.

7. *Caractères*, I, 198.

8. In *Miscellanies. The Last Volume*. See Ault and Butt, pp. 48-49.

Cibber in the revised *Dunciad* ("industrious Bug"), for Sappho in the *Epistle to a Lady* ("Insects that in muck begun"), and for Sporus. Dorset's lampoons and those written by his earlier contemporaries were ordinarily aimed at one or more particular people, not at a type. Subtlety of characterization would be out of place in such pieces. As a representation of character "Artimesia" is superior to "Phryne," but both have some kinship with the crude depictions in the satires of Shippen, Denham, Marvell, and others printed in the *New Collection of Poems Relating to State Affairs* which Pope read so attentively.

Precisely where to draw the line between the lampoon and the hostile incisive portrait it is not always possible to say. In Restoration satire the free application of withering epithets, sometimes in a train, may occur in either sort of writing. The cruder the attack, the more likely the resort to insulting epithet. "How easy it is," remarked Dryden in the Discourse prefixed to the *Satires*, "to call rogue and villain, and that wittily. But how hard to make a man appear a fool, a blockhead, or a knave, without using any of those opprobrious terms!" The easier method Dryden did not absolutely eschew; the younger Shaftesbury, he says, is "that unfeather'd two-legg'd thing, a Son," and of Shadwell (Og) he writes, "For ev'ry inch that is not Fool is Rogue."

Lesser poets called names with less inhibition. Somerset (Moro), says Shippen, is "A Stamm'ring, Hot, Conceited, Laughing" lord, and Halifax (Bathilo) is

> A gay, pragmatical, pretending Tool,
> Opinionatively wise, and pertly dull.
> A Demy-Statesman, Talkative, and Loud,
> Hot without Courage, without Merit proud.

In the Earl of Peterborough's collection of "Nine Worthies" is John Churchill, the future Duke of Marlborough, an "Ungrateful Toad-stool, despicable thing"; someone else, perhaps Danby, is called "a Jackanapes of State/ A Monkey turn'd into a Magistrate." Rochester refers *en passant* to "A Parliament of Knaves and Sots," and another poet writes about Chett,

> that Scoundrel, he who Nature Made,
> An arrant Fool, although a Rogue by Trade.

"Advice to a Painter, 1697" directs our eyes:

> See where the Florid Warlike C-tts appears
> As Brave and Senseless as the Sword he wears.[9]

This rough and styptic method of characterization, hurrying the reader along before he has time to consider, was adopted by Pope only infrequently. A few of his one-line decapitations employ it, and the word "Fool" is tellingly placed in the sketches of Wharton, Villiers, and Atossa. "Dunce" brings the account of Philomede to an end in a blow. It is in the scorching account of Sporus that one sees the full effect of this legacy from the lampoon—Sporus "that Thing of silk," "that mere white Curd of Ass's milk," "this Bug with gilded wings, / This painted Child of Dirt," a "Cherub's face, a Reptile all the rest." The more important part of the sketch, the real characterizing, is not in these phrases; they contribute chiefly hatred.

Even when Pope drew pictures of Atticus and Atossa, subjects that aroused in him a good deal of feeling, he preferred a more ample and analytical method of condemnation. A comparison with Dryden again will help. When Dryden was drawing Achitophel and Zimri he stood outside his subjects as the lampooner does; though he neither railed nor hurled epithets at these men, he was only the external observer, evaluating what he saw as any other shrewd spectator might do. Pope, on the other hand, somehow moves inward; he alternates description and impersonation. Watching Addison's tactics, he begins to feel his jealousy; watching his hesitations, he senses his disappointment. Yet Pope's hostility remains. Atossa, a more extravagant subject, requires a livelier description, but Pope makes us share the energy, the whirl of passion within the creature, her hatred of herself for yielding, her uncontrolled, uncontrollable starts of rage and longing. *Absalom and Achitophel* is a narrative poem, and hence Dryden,

---

9. These passages are culled from Pope's copy of *A New Collection of Poems Relating to State Affairs.*

reserving for the narrative sections of his work the expression of the feelings of his *dramatis personae,* never puts so much emotional experience within a character-sketch. But the scheme of the epistle allows Pope to reveal within the sketch a character's passions as well as his story.

Compare Dryden on Zimri—

> Railing and praising were his usual Theams;
> And both (to shew his Judgment) in Extreams:
> So over Violent, or over Civil,
> That every Man, with him, was God or Devil—

and Pope on Atossa—

> Her ev'ry turn with Violence pursu'd,
> Nor more a storm her Hate than Gratitude,
>
> .   .   .   .
>
> Love, if it makes her yield, must make her hate:
> Superiors? death! and Equals? what a curse!
> But an Inferior not dependant? worse.
> Offend her, and she knows not to forgive;
> Oblige her, and she'll hate you while you live.

These lines and those for Philomede, for Flavia, for Cloe, and for Atticus possess the energetic movement of a good lampoon and the psychological revelation of a good Character.

Sheffield was neither a Dryden nor a Pope, but his *Essay upon Satyr,* which Dryden helped polish and Pope later edited, could teach both poets something about the craft of combining in one sketch the observer's adverse comments with the subject's inner experience. The silencing epithet is rare in his poem except when he handles Chancellor Finch and the Earl of Rochester; they are his Sporus. The opposite fault of diffuseness is more common. His epithets are relatively gentle: Shaftesbury is "That nimblest Creature of the busie kind," Sedley a "night-bird chirping." George Savile, Earl and later Marquis of Halifax, is drawn in a typically mild and frank way, sympathy somehow implying an answer to the attack:

As the new Earl with parts deserving praise,
And wit enough to laugh at his own ways;
Yet loses all soft days and sensual nights,
Kind Nature checks, and kinder Fortune slights;
Striving against his quiet all he can,
For the fine Notion of a busie Man;
And what is that at best, but one whose mind,
Is made to tire himself and all mankind;
For Ireland he would go, faith let him reign,
For if some odd fantastick Lord would fain
Carry in Trunks, and all my drudgery do,
I'll not only pay him but admire him too;
But is there any other Beast that lives,
Who his own harm so wittily contrives?
Will any Dog that has his Teeth and Stones,
Refin'dly leave his Bitches and his Bones?
To turn a wheel, and bark to be employ'd,
While Venus is by rival Dogs enjoy'd;
Yet this fond Man to get a Statesman's Name,
Forfeits his Friends, his Freedom and his Fame.[10]

Sheffield tries to indicate the life within a man: Sedley awaiting supper, his greatest delight; Sheffield himself gladly escaping the marriage noose; and Buckingham helpless and happy before any proffered joke. Dryden says that Shaftesbury was "Sagacious, Bold, and Turbulent of wit," harboring

A fiery Soul, which working out its way,
Fretted the Pigmy Body to decay.

Sheffield describes Shaftesbury's body a little more plainly ("His Limbs are crippled, and his Body shakes") and, seeing into the man a little farther, he explains his state of mind more particularly:

---

10. Quoted from the text in *The Fourth (and Last) Collection of Poems* (1689), p. 29, apparently the first printing of the *Essay upon Satyr.*

> 'Twere Crime in any Man but him alone,
> To use a Body so, though 'tis ones own:
> Yet this false comfort never gives him o're,
> That whilst he creeps his vigorous thoughts can soar.[11]

In his poem Sheffield attempts, although not always successfully, to carry out the principles enunciated in his opening lines:

> In this alone me-thinks the Ancients err'd;
> Against the grossest Follies they disclaim,
> Hard they pursue, but hunt ignoble Game.
> Nothing is easier than such blots to hit,
> And 'tis the Talent of each vulgar Wit.

But our poet would seek

> with sharp Eyes those nicer faults to find,
> Which lye obscurely in the wisest Mind;
> That little speck, which all the rest does spoil.

The doctrine sounds promising, and all three poets wrote their best character-sketches when they were following it. Mr. Bickerstaff in *Tatler* Number 64 reveals that he had been instructed similarly: "The follies of the finest minds, which a philosophic surgeon knows how to dissect, will best employ your skill." Pope's Atossa if foolish is "The wisest Fool much Time has ever made," and all the other figures in the *Epistle to a Lady* that he devotes much attention to can pretend to some mind or merit. Of Addison, Villiers, Wharton, Bentley, Timon, and Marlborough the reader is made to feel that the same is true.

In each of his thirty Characters Theophrastus identifies at the outset what the nature of each type is[12] and then goes on, in illustration after illustration of behavior, to build up an image of the man.

---

11. Sheffield's "Character of Charles II," an interesting unrestrained analysis in prose, shows his ability in portraiture.

12. It is now thought that the initial sentences in the Characters may have been Byzantine additions, but because the sentences were always printed as part of the sketches, we may ignore the question of origin.

Our pleasure comes from recognizing the authentic, if also every-day, signs. As long as an author portrays types and we are not tired of the types chosen, this will be a successful method. Flattery, Theophrastus writes, "might be understood to be a sort of converse that is dishonourable, but at the same time profitable, to him that flatters; and the Flatterer will say as he walks beside you 'Are you aware how people are looking at you? No man in Athens gets such attention' . . . . And while he says such things as these, he picks a speck from your coat . . . . He will desire silence when his friend speaks . . . and if he make a stale jest will laugh, and stuff the corner of his cloak in his mouth as if he could not hold his merriment . . . ."[13] And so on. Theophrastus has caught for all time the salient gestures of the type—and in flattery the outer expression is everything. The passage of two thousand years has not weakened the force of this sketch, and in countless representations of the flatterer in writings of the seventeenth and eighteenth centuries the details of this picture variously reappear. Eventually seventeenth-century Character-writers were forced by the threat of triteness into choosing less and less familiar categories of humankind. Surprise in the illustrative detail became inevitable, and from novelty the reader now drew his satisfaction.

Along with greater unfamiliarity in the subject came a suitable change in technique. La Bruyère at the end of the century, scattering Characters of all sorts of upper-class people among his *pensées*, usually abandoned the Theophrastan opening definition and instead offered in his first sentence only half a hint or no hint at all of what the essence of his figure would be. Some of his Characters, Giton and Phedon particularly, are absolute riddles until we reach the final sentences. A great many of the people portrayed are unusual and individual, and for these the method of deliberate, gradual revelation is a good one. Yet La Bruyère so frequently forces the reader to remain in suspense that in spite of his extraordinary cleverness the manner sometimes becomes an annoying mannerism.

---

13. *The Characters of Theophrastus,* ed. and transl. by J. M. Edmonds, Loeb Classical Library (1929), pp. 43-45.

Pope, a more varied artist, adopts both plans and modifies each. Better at deductive than inductive procedures,[14] he often follows the example of Theophrastus in dealing with plain types. As Coleridge said, "in Pope's Timon, &c. the first two or three couplets contain all the pith of the character, and the twenty or thirty lines that follow are so much evidence . . . of overt acts of jealousy, or pride, or whatever it may be that is satirised."[15] Under Coleridge's "&c." we may include especially the depictions of the retired happy man in the "Ode on Solitude" and *Windsor Forest,* the blockhead critic in the *Essay on Criticism,* the unselfish country gentleman described just following Timon, the fop-patron in the *Epistle to Dr. Arbuthnot,* and Aristarchus. Yet two other type-figures, the miser Cotta and the avaricious Sir John Blunt in the *Epistle to Lord Bathurst,* are made interesting by a delaying presentation, in both cases ironic. In fact the eighteen-line passage allotted to "Much injur'd Blunt" (and the prophecy of universal corruption that led him, "Nobly wishing Party Rage to cease," to buy both parties) needs explanation, and in the octavo *Works* of 1735 Pope added an explanatory footnote.

In dealing with more individualized subjects Pope sometimes used the Theophrastan opening, sometimes La Bruyère's meandering approach. Wharton's ruling passion, Cloe's heartlessness, Atossa's constant arrogance and belligerence are stated at the outset, though to stop there would be as nonsensical as to stop with Theophrastus's saying that the flatterer indulges in a dishonorable activity profitable to himself. For the depiction of people as involuted and baffling as Sylvia, Calypso, Flavia, and Joseph Addison it is obvious that La Bruyère furnishes better models of procedure than Theophrastus. But in these drawings Pope substitutes for La Bruyère's continual sarcasm a modicum of wonder and even of regret.

A feature of Restoration satire that one becomes conscious of as one reads is the bad habit, perhaps left over from mid-century polemics, of ascribing the same faults and too many faults to everyone.

---

14. Donald A. Stauffer, *The Nature of Poetry* (New York, 1946) pp. 128-130, 249.

15. *Specimens of the Table Talk of Samuel Taylor Coleridge* (1851), p. 192.

Each man, whatever else his category, is likely sooner or later to be dubbed fool or knave, each woman in some fashion whore. Dryden's depiction of Gilbert Burnet as the Buzzard in *The Hind and the Panther* illustrates this sort of indiscriminate abuse in a more sophisticated form. Burnet, we read, is a brawny carnal priest, a wit, a self-seeking conscienceless parasite, venomous, blasphemous, both artfully "Nice" and carelessly crude, "Invulnerable in his Impudence," a revealer of the secrets of confession, and

> So fond of loud Report, that not to miss
> Of being known (his last and utmost bliss)
> He rather would be known, for what he is.

One could not expect Dryden to present Burnet's ideal of a broad Church in a sympathetic way or to evaluate his intelligence, courage, and honesty as we now can; but one could hope that he would produce a picture that is better unified and more plausible. As it stands, the sketch of the Buzzard consists partly of references to special actions with obscure meanings of their own and partly of broadly damning charges that would fit many kinds of objectionable people. The portrait is blurred by the abuse.

Pope's depictions of Sporus and of the man made out of Donne's Coscus likewise suggest the unrestraint of the lampoon; in the case of Sporus the author's anger, though intense and fluent, has not destroyed the outline of the figure. But Donne's young lawyer who makes love in legal jargon is obscured in Pope's final version (ll. 45-62) by a splatter of faults; he is wealthy, pert, proud, a bad poet, even perhaps a criminal, and courts women in financial language as well as in the rough terms of the courts of law. Pope's adding gross carnality to Horace's miser in the new character Fufidia and ghoulishness to his miser Avidienus and his substituting nasty pox for the poison dispensed by Horace's sorceress (*Sat.*, II, i, 48) also place him in the tradition either of Juvenal or the English lampoon.

It should be remarked that one common method of the lampoon Pope usually rejects. This is the utilizing of a man's personal appearance in a character-portrayal. To see what is involved in this rejection we need to consider several matters.

In the old-fashioned Character not much use could be made of a man's external aspect, for the types originally presented were moral or psychological. Yet the white teeth and frequent hair-cut of Theophrastus's Man of Petty Vanity, the foreign dress and pick-tooth of Overbury's Affected Traveller and the wrinkled skin and driveled beard of his Old Man, the crossed arms and missing hatband of Earle's Discontented Man, the fresh complexion, fat cheeks, and bold eye of La Bruyère's rich man Giton—in such cases a view of the subject's appearance helps to suggest his nature and define his class. Will Honeycomb's unwrinkled brow (*Spectator* No. 2) and the Political Upholsterer's scowl and rags (*Tatler* No. 155) serve the same purpose. But these examples I have found only after searching; the figure and dress of a person as distinguished from his gestures, words, and deeds, are not important in the methods of Theophrastus, Hall, Earle, La Bruyère, Steele, and Addison.

But in the depiction of historical individuals one might suppose the opportunities would be greater. "The Portrait has this advantage of the Character," Flecknoe pointed out in 1660, "that it gives you the Bodies resemblance together with the disposition of the Mind; and the Writer of the Painter, that he both depaints the Minde, and Body too."[16] In France in the middle years of the seventeenth century the composition of pen-portraits was for a time a popular entertainment. In the romances of La Calprenède a formula emerged for a description including specific details about hair, proportions of the face, eyes, mouth, complexion, neck, hands, bearing, gait; and the formula could be adapted to the depiction of living persons. It served the *précieux* habitués of the salons when they composed flattering portraits of each other. It was refined and varied by Mlle de Scudéry in the idealized representations of some of these same people in her sumptuous romances, particularly *Le Grand Cyrus* and *Clélie*.

Richard Flecknoe hoped to bring the portrait into fashion in England, and offered the following picture of Charles II, "Faithfully

16. *Heroick Portraits*, Preface.

taken to the Life," as the first in his *Heroick Portraits.* I quote only
about a third of the whole, but the reader will have the heart of the
picture and perhaps enough of Flecknoe's verse.

> His Person's such, as he for that alone
> (His Birth away) deserves the Royal Throne;
> Such Majesty there's in it . . .
>
> .   .   .   .
>
> His Stature's tall, and of the comliest make,
> His Visage oval, his Hair thick and black,
> In ample Curles, on's shoulders falling down,
> Adorning more his Head, then any Crown.
> His Eyes are Lively, full of flame and sprite,
> And of that colour most delights the sight:
>
> .   .   .   .
>
> He knows what e're befits a Prince to know;
> Not learnt from th'dead, but from the world, & men,
>
> .   .   .   .
>
> For moral vertues then, ha's every one
> In their full splendors and perfection,
> Justice, not Clouded with severity,
> Nor Temperance, with sower austerity;
> And ne're in none more Courage was, nor more
> Wisdom and Prudence, with less vanity, nor
> With lesser Artifice; then ore's passion he
> Commands so absolutely, and sovereignly:
> It shews him King over himself . . .
>
> .   .   .   .
>
> . . . nor does he less excell
> In civil vertues, which adorn no less
> The Royal Throne, as mildness, Gentleness,
> Ravishing sweetness, debonarity,
>
> .   .   .   .
>
> Nor yet could all his troubles nor his cares
> Render him less gay and chearful, which declares

His minde above them all . . .

. . . . . .

Knows Musick, Poetry, Gallantry, and Wit,
And none knows better how to judge of it:

. . . .

. . . .

But of all Titles, that amongst the rest,
Of Gratious and Clement fits him best . . . .

For reasons which we can perhaps in part supply, Flecknoe did not succeed in his desire to popularize the courtly portrait in England. In France La Bruyère broke away from this flattering manner almost entirely. Yet when he was sketching Aemile, recognized by everyone as his patron the great Condé, he omitted any reference to the ugly teeth and eagle-like profile that might somehow have been used to give a fuller impression of a man whose personality in his later years must have been disagreeable. In his characterizations of La Fontaine ("grossier, lourd"), Corneille ("timide"), and Santeuil ("un enfant en cheveux gris") he offered a hint or two of physical appearance but no more. Like Steele and Addison after him he did not make the subjects of his portraits, whether pleasant or otherwise, physically recognizable. The handful of sketches in the *Tatler* and the *Spectator* that can now be safely said to have been portraits, such as the pictures of Sir John Holt (Verus) in *Tatler* Number 14, of Atterbury in Number 66, and of Robert Molesworth in Number 189, indicate the quality of the man's mind or his moral nature or behavior, not his appearance. These authors are interested in certain phenomena of character, the meaning of the person as the writer at the moment sees it, rather than in the man's particular *tout ensemble*. Even Clarendon and Burnet, who name their subjects and are writing history rather than moral essays or *pensées*, say relatively little about physical features, though Burnet is less niggardly than Clarendon with such information.

But the satirists of the Restoration, if also concerned with "history," had stronger passions than the historians allowed themselves, and their manners were different. Consequently the people discussed in *A New Collection of Poems Relating to State Affairs* are made as unpleasant to look at as they are to think about. Andrew Marvell's "Last Instructions to a Painter" directs the artist to paint the black hair, big limbs, and red face of Sir Thomas Daniel; the wide mouth, oyster lip, and big belly and rump of the Duchess of York; and Henry Jermyn's elephantine chin. Sheffield, though more genial in his *Essay upon Satyr* than many of these authors, none the less points at Shaftesbury's crippled limbs, shaking body, and feeble legs. Outside of the *New Collection* the same habits obtain; one may think of the graphic presentation of Thomas Shadwell and Titus Oates in *Absalom and Achitophel,* of Burnet in *The Hind and the Panther.*

Though there was, then, some authority for characterization by means of physical description, one notices that Pope usually avoided it. Perhaps it was sensitiveness about his own miserable body that turned his attention away from this method—except in references to Sylvia's low-cut gown, Artimesia's huge body and unpared fingernails, Sappho's dirty smock, Calypso's eyes, the vast bulk and flat eyes of Moore-Smythe, and the painted white face of Hervey (Sporus). Hervey's epilepsy he did not mention.

Again we should recall that Pope spent more than a year in the studio of Charles Jervas trying to learn to paint portraits in oil and "from the canvas call the mimic face" as he said Jervas did.[17] The work of Jervas's master, the great court-painter Sir Godfrey Kneller, Pope studied along with that of his friend. Kneller, Pope said in an epitaph, was a painter "Whose Art was Nature, and whose Pictures thought," and although he later referred to this epitaph as "the worst thing I ever wrote,"[18] it was probably not the idea at the end of this line (which he borrowed from Dryden) that gave him discontent so much as the extravagance of several other lines. For in spite of one's impression that the majority of Kneller's faces are far from thoughtful, some of them are most expressive; one would give more than

<hr>

17. "Epistle to Mr. Jervas, With Dryden's Translation of Fresnoy's Art of Painting."
18. Ault and Butt, p. 313.

the proverbial penny for the thoughts behind the unexpectedly sensitive and pensive face of his John Locke, the proud and critical face of his Matthew Prior, and the mellow, quizzical, penetrating gaze of his John Evelyn. One would barter all the "Beauties" and all the Kit-Kat series for these. The painting of Kneller's that Pope must have studied especially is that of Thomas Betterton, for his own painting of Betterton seems to have been based upon it.[19] It is not one of Kneller's deeper works. Perhaps an actor's face in repose is usually not interesting. Betterton had been a neighbor of Pope's, and the poet doubtless copied the Kneller portrait at least partly for sentimental reasons.

What eventually caused Pope to abandon painting in oils is anyone's guess. But a hint may possibly be drawn from his couplets on Kneller's portrait of the charming, intellectual, and altogether individual young matron, Lady Mary Wortley Montagu. The lines, written probably about six years after Pope left Jervas's studio, are as follows:

> The play full smiles around the dimpled mouth
> That happy air of Majesty and Youth.
> So would I draw (but oh, 'tis vain to try
> My narrow Genius does the power deny)
> The Equal Lustre of the Heavenly mind
> Where every grace with every Virtue's join'd
> Learning not vain, and wisdom not severe
> With Greatness easy, and with wit sincere.
> With Just Description shew the Soul Divine
> And the whole Princesse in my work should shine.[20]

Although it is not quite clear what Pope meant to imply about Kneller's achievement in the portrait, one might safely infer, at least, that Pope was saying that the most difficult part of the painter's task is to depict the mind, not the face.[21] His *Epistle to a Lady* starts as a

---

19. See above p. 43 and Appendix A.
20. Ault and Butt, pp. 211-212.
21. Robert Halsband, *Life of Lady Mary Wortley Montagu* (Oxford, 1956), p. 99, interprets the lines as expressive of complete satisfaction with the picture.

set of paintings of women distinguishable from each other by their costumes and facial expression: Arcadia's countess in ermined pride, then as a shepherdess; Fannia as the leering, loving wife and then as naked Leda; a Magdalen; a St. Cecilia; Flavia in diamonds and a dirty smock. But in this *Epistle* and indeed in other poems Pope abandons such obvious things and moves on to the kind of work he could do better and by which he might reasonably hope to remain famous—the sharp, firm, penetrating sketches of minds (not often heavenly) and of souls (rather less than divine).

The most interesting figures in Pope's gallery are those given psychological portraits; the physical appearance of most of them is unimportant, especially when, as in the case of Addison, appearances are understood to be deliberately deceptive or when, as in the case of Wharton, motive seems unrelated to behavior. Furthermore, if the subject to be portrayed was a simple type—the frugal crone, the spend-thrift, the vain woman, or the glutton—Pope apparently thought he could achieve greater force in a dramatic presentation than in a merely visual description. There is one portrait, however, which he might have improved by attending, as the painter does, to the subject's face and figure. This is the sketch of Marlborough, whose extraordinary handsomeness could have been used to explain what Pope regarded as his unmerited rise and his empty, evil success.

Yet one cannot seriously wish even in this case that Pope had tried literally to duplicate the painter's art in words. In spite of Horace's *ut pictura poesis*, the two arts are not the same. But for half a century French and English theorists had been attending to the idea advanced by both Aristotle and Quintilian that men's passions could be known by their outward signs.[22] Charles Le Brun, one of the painters at the court of Louis XIV, obligingly provided a text-book with a set of simple drawings to show what happens to the face under the stress of each emotion. Scorn, he explains (I quote from the English translation of 1701, which was dedicated to Kneller),

---

22. See Brewster Rogerson's interesting and important discussion of this subject, "The Art of Painting the Passions," *Journal of the History of Ideas*, XIV (1953), 68-94.

"is expressed by the Eye-brow frowning and drawn down by the side of the Nose, the other end thereof very much raised; the Eye very open, and the Eye-ball in the middle; the Nostrils drawn upwards; the Mouth shut, the Corners a little drawn down; and the under Lip thrust out beyond the upper."[23] Mercifully there is a vigorous line-drawing to accompany each analysis, and Le Brun thus proves his analysis correct. But what reader could see Scorn, with the eye-ball in the middle, as readily in the words as in the drawing? Besides, Le Brun's patterns deal with the several passing emotions, not with fundamental character, which he apparently felt unequal to codifying.

Just the year before Pope died, an English writer published a curious "Essay on the Knowledge of the Characters of Men" which proposed a few rules for identifying basic character by the appearance of the face as well as by a man's behavior. The essay is really no more promising on this subject than Le Brun's analyses. The author, who had just published an irresistible study of human nature called *The History of the Adventures of Joseph Andrews, and of his Friend Mr. Abraham Adams,* declares it possible to discover the essential nature of a man from his appearance provided one does not mis-understand the signs. Austerity or gravity of countenance usually indicates only "Pride, Ill-nature, and Cunning."[24] A fierce aspect reveals a bully whereas true courage is shown by a "fiery Cast of the Eyes," not by a "strong Contraction of the Muscles." A genuinely good heart expresses itself in an "amiable, open, composed, cheerful Aspect." A "constant, settled, glavering, sneering Smile in the Coun-tenance" should never be mistaken, as it often is, for a sign of good nature; rather, it comes from a "Compound of Malice and Fraud" and betokens "a bad Heart." All this may be the soundest physiog-nomy, and the faces of the characters in Fielding's novels, one recalls, are sometimes described in such phrases as these. But the projection of Fielding's creations depends relatively little upon facial descrip-tions.[25] Nor does Parson Adams's excited argument with his skeptical

---

23. *The Conference of Monsieur LeBrun . . . Upon Expression* (1701), p. 16.
24. Henry Fielding, *Miscellanies* (1743), I, 188-189.
25. In *Joseph Andrews* there are several satiric thrusts and comic moments due

host about the possibility of recognizing the "portraiture of the mind in the countenance" (II, xvii) prove much. Fielding and Pope agree that most people cannot read character very well. As I have indicated, Pope says almost nothing about facial expression and very little about the bodily form or the dress or the look of a character.

It may be noticed in passing that the title of Fielding's "Essay on the Knowledge of the Characters of Men" is a sort of corrected version of the alternate or sub-title of Pope's *Epistle to Lord Cobham*, "Of the Knowledge and Characters of Men." Although Fielding quotes Pope late in the essay, it is one of his letters that is quoted. The first part of the essay, however, seems like a commentary on ideas expressed in the *Epistle* to Cobham. Pope's saying that "There's some Peculiar in each leaf and grain" as well as in each man is matched by Fielding's analogy between the inborn peculiarity or "Genius of a Tree, that it will flourish so many Years, loves such a Soil, bears such a Fruit, &c." and the inborn "original Difference" between the natures of one child and another. Ignoring the question, important to Pope, of man's perpetual changing from himself, Fielding agrees with Pope that some men "are open, and to all men known," that others overdo their calculation and pretence and are "hid from none." Pope's discussion of the fact that "Not always Actions shew the man" and yet that "Actions best discover man" is shaped to lead to his theory of the key or ruling passion. Fielding considers the question much more solemnly, arguing that how a man behaves to the people closest to him will indicate his quality as his public behavior will not. Pope's illustration of the problem—the Tsar (later changed to Caesar) in military retreat or risking all for a woman—is more flamboyant than serious; Fielding, on the contrary, treats the question as it would arise in ordinary life. It is in this

to the discrepancy between appearances and real character: Lady Booby misunderstands Joseph's blushes; Tim the hosteler is a lamb who looks like a lion (I, xi); Leonora's face shows good humor, often mistaken for good nature (II, iv); a hostess shows generosity not because her nature, in spite of her sour face, is generous but because she thinks Adams has resources from which to repay her. See also *Tom Jones*, VIII, iv. Sophia Western is one of the few characters in *Tom Jones* whose faces are carefully described (IV, ii), but Fielding does not indicate that her face reveals her mind.

connection that he introduces Pope's query, "How shall a Man love five Millions, who could never love a single Person?"[26] As if by way of compliment to the *Epistle to a Lady* (called *Of the Characters of Women* in the full title of the first edition), Fielding explains somewhat ostentatiously that all his remarks apply to men only, "the Knowledge of the Characters of Women being . . . a Science, to which I make not the least Pretension."[27] But he ignores altogether Pope's enthusiastically presented notion that only a knowledge of the ruling passion will allow one to see into the nature of each man. No such elaborate means is necessary, according to Fielding, whose question in every case is simply whether a man is honest and moral or whether he is not. Eventually in his last novel, *Amelia*, Fielding faced the more complicated psychological and philosophical issues involved in Pope's doctrine and condemned any faith in or surrender to a ruling passion as destructive of religion and happiness.[28]

Although Pope does little with physical appearance as a means of vivifying his figures, he sometimes employs a background-scene for this purpose. Theophrastus affords momentary glimpses of market-place, theater, streets, or baths, but there are no full views. Likewise Hall, Overbury, and Earle keep the background fragmentary. Horace, Juvenal, and Boileau evoke scenes somewhat more generously, but except for the plentiful detail in Horace's second Epode I recall no picture of a place so carefully organized in these three poets as Pope's of the silent empty hall of the miser Cotta in the *Epistle to Lord Bathurst*. Pope's most striking revelation of character by means of a scene is, of course, the large and lavish painting of

26. Fielding's *Miscellanies*, I, 223. The sentence is quoted from one of Pope's extravagant letters to Fielding's kinswoman, Lady Mary Wortley Montagu, in print since 1735. See *Correspondence*, I, 357.

27. Fielding's observation (*Tom Jones*, XIV, i) that women of the highest society are "so entirely made up of Form and Affectation, that they have no Character at all, at least, none which appears," could easily be taken as a kind of public agreement with the opening of Pope's *Epistle*.

28. For a full analysis of Fielding's views on this subject see the unpublished doctoral dissertation of LeRoy W. Smith, "The Doctrine of the Passions as It Appears in the Works of Henry Fielding, Particularly in *Amelia*" (Duke University, 1956).

Timon's villa in the *Epistle to Lord Burlington.* Parterre and slopes and statues and fountains, library and chapel and marble dining-room gorgeously proclaim the pride and heartlessness of their owner. Here and in Book IV of the *Dunciad* the descriptive poet is given as much freedom as the satirist of character, with delightful results.

A form of sketch common in the historians, ancient and modern, combines biography and the analysis of personality. An inevitable sort of thing, it can be as long as Clarendon's account of Lord Falkland, Sheffield's and Halifax's "Characters" of Charles II, or as short as an epitaph, and as delightfully droll as numerous such brief "lives" in the *Tatler* and *Spectator.* Pope's unfailing variety and inventiveness appear in his productions of this sort. There is his account of Sir Balaam in the *Epistle to Lord Bathurst.* Though a "tale" as Pope says rather than a character-sketch, its deft revelation of Sir Balaam's ideas and feelings as he easily slips down the moral ladder in order to gain economic and social advantages is masterly. Another variation of the biographical summary is that most brilliant passage, the picture in *Dunciad* Book IV of the career and character of the young aristocrat, home from the Grand Tour. What makes the passage so successful, besides the elegant suppleness of the language and the beauty of the sybaritic vision, is the neat geographical progress matching the youth's progress through time into folly and vice. The lines also have the *éclat* of a public oration.

Something of the same splendid manner, but with appropriate changes of tone, Pope attempted in his biographical sketches of Kyrle, Villiers, Wharton, and Marlborough. The sketch of Kyrle is the loosest in organization. To arouse admiration for the Christian benevolence of the Man of Ross (and to entertain the reader) Pope evokes grand images of the hoarse river Severn, of woods hanging upon mountains, of clear waters flowing from the rock through the plain. After these, to stimulate pity and generosity, Pope offers equally brief glimpses of an alms-house, apprenticed orphans, the sick room. Kyrle himself, as I have remarked before, is realized only impersonally and vaguely as the invisible cause of all this.

Contrasted in every respect is the sketch that follows of George Villiers, the wild Duke of Buckingham.[29] Its first part is anything but grand—an exact description in seven lines of "the worst inn's worst room." After this intimate beginning come quick glimpses of Buckingham's fine, sequestered palace at Cliveden and of a Privy Council meeting with the merry King. Four mournful lines sweep the story to its ironic end before Pope goes back to construct a further personal view of Buckingham in conversation with a parsimonious rich businessman. The Benevolent Man appears in the poem as an abstract ideal; the Noble Rake is a clear, individual case before our eyes.

That rhetoric comes naturally to the writer of epitaphs and biographical character-sketches is made less obvious by Pope's treatment of Kyrle and Villiers than of Wharton and Marlborough. Pope displays the natures of the latter men against the background of their great opportunities. Many particular portions of Wharton's career are alluded to, and the poet's exclamations play ironically over the psychology of his subject. On the other hand, the life and character of Marlborough are sketched only summarily, but Pope's moral disapproval heightens every remark. The dirt, seaweed, laurels, and gold summoned to mind like an escutcheon at the beginning, the trophied arches and storied halls seen midway in the sketch, and the image, near the end, of the coffin born aloft amidst dry pomps by "regardless Vet'rans"—Pope's lines are splendid, funereal, clangorous.

The purpose of the epitaph—and such is the nature of the sketch of Marlborough—is to say something compendious and solemn, and this leads to general phrases and a grand manner. The result can be memorable, but it is very rarely a revealing, reliable portrait. Pope's epitaph on his friend Elijah Fenton seems one of the better ones; yet there is a sentence about Fenton in Pope's letter to Broome that speaks of his amiable nature and that is needed to give a complete impression of what Pope thought about him.[30]

---

29. See the excellent analysis of this sketch in Robert W. Rogers, *The Major Satires of Alexander Pope*, in *Illinois Studies in Lang. and Lit.*, XL (Urbana, 1955), 62-63, and the added Vergilian reference in Reuben A. Brower, *Alexander Pope* (Oxford, 1959), p. 257.

30. Ault and Butt, p. 319 n.; *Correspondence*, III, 128.

The epitaphs most nearly constituting portraits are those of Dorset and Gay. The lines "On Charles Earl of Dorset" are as follows:

> Dorset, the Grace of Courts, the Muses Pride,
> Patron of Arts, and Judge of Nature, dy'd!
> The Scourge of Pride, tho' sanctify'd or great,
> Of Fops in Learning, and of Knaves in State:
> Yet soft his Nature, tho' severe his Lay,
> His Anger moral, and his Wisdom gay.
> Blest Satyrist! who touch'd the Mean so true,
> As show'd, Vice had his hate and pity too.
> Blest Courtier! who could King and Country please,
> Yet sacred keep his Friendships, and his Ease.
> Blest Peer! his great Forefathers ev'ry Grace
> Reflecting, and reflected in his Race;
> Where other Buckhursts, other Dorsets shine,
> And Patriots still, or Poets, deck the Line.[31]

Here in brief are suggestions of the manners, attitudes, instincts, interests, professional career, and literary accomplishments of the subject. The picture, needless to say, is flattering; only in a phrase or two does it hint that this could be the man that Sheffield had painted many years earlier as "Drinking all night, and dozing all the day."[32] Pope's estimate of his satires as warmed with pity and touching "the Mean" seems justified neither by Dorset's poems nor by Pope's imitations of them. Yet the epitaph is successful as a composed portrait.

The epitaph on John Gay for Westminster Abbey is a montage of type-images. Swiftly reminding us of innocent child, man of wit, easy friend, humble man, incorruptible gentleman, and moral satirist, it affords a tentative outline of an individual. The verses are appealing because the subject is. But to anyone not acquainted with Gay's life

---

31. *The Works of Mr. Alexander Pope. Volume II* (1735), fol., "Epitaphs," pp. 4-5.

32. It was from this sketch in the *Essay upon Satyr* that Pope probably derived a hint for the line "Chaste to her Husband, frank to all beside" in his picture of Philomede in the *Epistle to a Lady*. Sheffield had said that Dorset foolishly married "A teeming Widow but a barren Wife."

and writings, the picture could be no more than shadowy. The other epitaphs, including the somewhat descriptive ones on Withers, the brave humane soldier; on Mrs. Corbet and on Pope's father,[33] feminine and masculine examples of the modestly good type made familiar in countless earlier literary depictions; and on John Knight, Lord Caryll, and Sir William Trumbull, all equally virtuous, steady patriots—these do not increase Pope's stature as a portrait-painter, whatever they reveal of the vigor to be gained from crisp antithesis.[34] He is a master of the mood of retrospective sadness and of the summary phrase. But though author of about thirty epitaphs, he twice alluded to this sort of composition as "Flatteries and False History."[35]

One cannot conclude a survey of Pope's many kinds of character-sketches without paying one's respects to the successful arrangement of them in his five major epistles. The Jacobean and Caroline Character-books ordinarily assembled their sketches without much order; the plain division into virtuous types and evil types by Hall and Breton was not interesting and not often imitated, and the painting together of contrasted types—the courageous man and the craven, the good wife and the bad—was usually left to the sermons, manners-books, and other kinds of professional didacticism. La Bruyère adopted only loose groupings—women, the court, the fashionable, the wealthy, personal merit, etc.—that are not mutually exclusive. Young adopted the *omnium gatherum* method (except for sex) of the Character-books, Dryden placed portraits sparingly amidst narrative, and Sheffield in the *Essay upon Satyr* opened with abstract discourse followed by portraits in a cluster. In a letter to Tonson Pope said, speaking of the sketch of Kyrle in the then unfinished *Epistle to Lord Bathurst,* that "the manner in which it is placed, and the contrast (as the painters call it) in which it stands" produce whatever beauty it has in the poem.[36] Even if these words were perhaps a polite way of refusing to show Tonson parts of the poem until the whole work was properly finished, the principle Pope carried out effectively.

---

33. *Epistle to Dr. Arbuthnot*, ll. 392-403 (Butt).
34. See below pp. 127-128.
35. *Correspondence*, IV, 13; footnote on original *Dunciad*, I, 41.
36. *Correspondence*, III, 290.

The juxtaposing of Sabinus who loved woods and his son who preferred "One boundless Green" in the first *Epistle* (to Burlington) and miserly Cotta and his extravagant son in the second (to Bathurst) is an easy, natural way of stating contrasts, similar to the placement of the pictures of the bookful-blockhead critic and the good critic in the *Essay on Criticism* (derived from the similar contrast of sensible critic and mad poet in Horace's *Ars Poetica*).[37] All these sketches are the simplest outlines and they strengthen each other. The large painting of wasteful Timon in the first *Epistle* is expressively followed by a small one of the country squire who uses his money for the good of all. That poem is a pictorial affair; no subtleties of ethics or difficult notions of taste are to be grasped, and the design is obvious.[38]

In the second *Epistle* (to Bathurst) the thesis is more complicated,[39] and Pope's mind is dwelling on the particular problems and decisions of many men. Opening with conversational observations on single actions of numerous people, named and unnamed, the poem slows down slightly to suggest the pretended logic of Sir John Blunt. This passage is part of the fabric, droll and sarcastic, of the first section of the poem and is not meant as a full portrait. Then Pope gives us the classical miser and spendthrift son, the latter presented in an ironic revelation, modern in detail, to contrast with a semi-medieval picture of the old father. The Man of Ross and Villiers, opposites in character, are both presented with scenic material but in dissimilar fashion. The tale of Sir Balaam concludes fittingly a poem that on the surface seems rambling, anecdotal. Into Sir Balaam's story Pope deftly weaves psychological revelation more searching than that of Blunt and Cotta's son but similarly ironic. These caustic

37. Compare also Horace's placing two brothers together, one who prefers idle self-indulgence, the other who works untiringly to cultivate his farm-land (*Epistles,* II, ii, 183-186).

38. La Rochefoucauld's "Réflexion" entitled "Du Gout" might have given Pope some ideas for it; the division of people into five classes in respect to taste, of which the largest class (the one Pope begins with) consists of those who follow other people's taste, suggests a resemblance to a good many of Pope's ideas.

39. See Earl R. Wasserman, *Pope's Epistle to Bathurst: A Critical Reading* (Baltimore, 1960).

and ironic portions contrast with the less psychological, more pictorial treatments of Kyrle and Villiers.

The design of the third *Epistle* (to Cobham) seems simpler. The only important contrast is between the group of unfathomable people shown in the middle of the poem (as it was first published) and a set of familiar types at the end, the showpiece and center being the extended analysis of Wharton. In *To a Lady* and in the *Arbuthnot* a contrast is established between many kinds of objectionable people and an idealized figure (three idealized figures of the Pope family in the *Arbuthnot*) climactically placed at the end. In *To a Lady* this arrangement is part of Pope's very pretty adaptation of the plan of the seventeenth-century "Advice to a Painter" poems, of which there were ten in the *New Collection of Poems Relating to State Affairs.* Pope's epistle is, really, not a set of directions *to* a painter but a somewhat talkative painter's explanations delivered to an attentive lady on a tour of a portrait gallery. The fact that, after the first few pictures are passed, the poet-painter shows no interest in what the ladies look like is part of the humor of the work. Somewhere before the end (perhaps about line 207 [Bateson]) the poem becomes a written epistle, but the termination in a direct address to the lady preserves a common feature of the "Advice to a Painter" poems. Several of them, after prolonged satiric complaints, end in a special, serious address "To the King." One of them, "Directions to a Painter concerning the Dutch War: in 1667," concludes thus:

> And now, dear Painter, after pains, like those,
> 'Twere time that I and thou too do repose.

Pope's "complimentary close" is more courtly and yet exquisitely personal.[40]

A more complex organization has been thought to inhere in the defensive *Epistle to Dr. Arbuthnot;* Pope may have been deliberately spacing sketches there like an expert ancient rhetorician, preparing the audience to accept his praise of himself and his condemnation of

---

40. See Wallace Douglas, Roy Lamson, Hallett Smith, eds., *The Critical Reader* (New York, 1949), pp. 25-31, for an analysis of this poem.

his several enemies.[41] One sees that in all five poems Pope developed a form more orderly and meaningful than La Bruyère's and far more supple and shapely than Young's. Crowding elaborate character-sketches into each poem as Horace would ordinarily not do and bringing out the individualities of many of the figures more brightly, Pope created compositions of a new sort. They suggest something of the impression of movement through busy streets, as in the Roman satires, and something of the subdued buzz of conversation in an elegant drawing-room, as in La Bruyère. Only a writer acutely responsive to people and one stimulated by willing attendance upon social gatherings would write these poems, more "characteristical" than Horace's. Only an artist fascinated by the possibilities of form would create and arrange a collection of pictures so various in manner and design.

41. See Elder Olson, "Rhetoric and the Appreciation of Pope," *Modern Philol.*, XXXVII (1939), 13-35; Maynard Mack, "The Muse of Satire," *Yale Review*, XLI (1951-52), 80-92.

CHAPTER VI

The RULING PASSION *and the* COMPLEX PERSONALITY

IN 1730 Pope told Joseph Spence of a "New Hypothesis, That a prevailing passion in ye mind is brought wth it into ye world, & continues till death."[1] This hypothesis evidently was a special development from Pope's long-continued interest in the curious conformations of thought and emotion, of motive and pretense, of behavior and self-justification, of shrewdness and extravagance in men and women. Several of his early character-sketches had revealed his attention to human oddity, and it is not surprising that he should eventually formulate some general principles about human nature. The "new" hypothesis he was to expound in the second Book of the *Essay on Man*, where he treated also the larger question of how the inescapable passions are related to mental life and moral character. As for the "Master Passion in the Breast," it is there described as coming into a man with his first breath, swallowing up the lesser passions. It flows into his whole life and being, absorbing each "vital humour."

> Nature its Mother, Habit is its Nurse;
> Wit, Spirit, Faculties, but make it worse;
> Reason itself but gives it Edge and Pow'r,
> As Heav'ns blest Beam turns Vinegar more sow'r.

In the *Epistle to Lord Cobham* Pope expatiated further on the nature of the ruling passion:

---

1. Quoted in Bateson, p. xxii, from the Spence manuscripts belonging to James M. Osborn.

In this one Passion Man can strength enjoy,
As Fits give vigour, just when they destroy.
Time, that on all things lays his lenient hand,
Yet tames not this: it sticks to our last sand.

In the *Epistle to Lord Bathurst* and the *Epistle to a Lady* the ruling passion is alluded to, though briefly and without any show of excitement. But for a time Pope seems to have found the "new" idea fascinating, and in the *Essay on Man* he enunciated it so strikingly that it echoed down the century in the writings of other authors.

Of course the notion that a predominant or central or unifying element exists within the emotional and moral character of each person was not new. In ancient times the humoral theory of anatomy and medicine had established a physical basis for such a notion; vestiges of the humors physiology and "adust complexion" can be seen in both of Pope's discussions of his new hypothesis. Various writers, some of them favorites with him, had expressed ideas that may have contributed to the shaping of his. Horace mentioned the attendant genius who governs a life and dies with it.[2] Montaigne said that everyone finds in himself a form of his own, a governing form ("une forme sienne, une forme maistresse"), that opposes the tempest of passions contrary to him.[3] Bacon's essay "Of Empire" alludes to the central desire that gives shape to some men's lives. Dryden's "Grounds of Criticism in Tragedy" includes the assertion that every character in drama should be drawn with one virtue, vice, or passion "predominant over all the rest." Others in Pope's day made minor use of the phrase "predominant passion" or "ruling passion."[4]

2. *Epist.*, II, ii, 187-189. Shaftesbury ("Advice to an Author," I, ii) says that the ancient idea is not to be taken literally.
3. Book III, chap. ii, "Du Repentir." Maynard Mack in the Introduction and the footnotes in his edition of the *Essay on Man* points out several of these passages paralleling Pope's.
4. See *The Secret History of the Duke of Alancon and Queen Elizabeth* (1691), p. 43; Roscommon's *Essay on Translated Verse*, l. 92; Prior's unpublished essay, "Opinion," which Pope may have read (*Literary Works of Matthew Prior*, ed H. Bunker Wright and Monroe K. Spears [Oxford, 1959], I, xxxii-xxxiii, 558); Steele, *The Christian Hero*, ed. Rae Blanchard (1932), p. 79.

Supporting these and doubtless many more references to such a conception was the venerable and explicit literary doctrine of Aristotle and Horace which assumed the existence of recognizable, seemingly universal types of character. Though Horace outside the *Ars Poetica* spoke more than once of man's changeable nature, he did not in these passages confuse changeability with permanent, mysterious complexity. Even if a man is unsteady, his stages as he is moved by one propensity after another are familiar and definable; the inconsistent man is *simply* inconsistent. As Addison said in *Spectator* Number 70, "Human Nature is the same in all reasonable Creatures," and neo-classical criticism had long since established the expectation that dramatis personae would be clear, definite, regular. Pope's hypothesis rested on a very ancient foundation; possibly what he said to Spence was not that the hypothesis was new but that his interest in it was. In either case, the prominence given to it in the poems he published in the earlier 1730's would lead one to suppose that the ruling passion would turn out to be important in the organization of his character-sketches, at least of that period, and that it would account to some extent for their success.

When one applies Pope's hypothesis to many of his pictures of standard sorts of people, one sees that it appears to be adequate and fair. The lecherous man, the frugal woman, the glutton Helluo and vain Narcissa, the polite courtier and penurious Euclio (in the *Epistle to Lord Cobham*), all dying just as they had lived, are clear victims of a prevailing passion. So are miserly Cotta, avaricious Blunt, pleasure-loving Villiers, and proudly ostentatious Timon. All this is plain and easy.

But there are in Pope's many poems certain type-characters, plausible enough as representatives of one class or another, for which the explanation of a congenital master-passion will not readily serve. What inborn passion could explain the calm, reasonable lover of innocent retirement portrayed in the early "Ode on Solitude"? What permanent, basic passion produced Sabinus's love of trees and shade and his son's delight in boundless open land? The carnation-fancier, the butterfly-collector, the materialistic philosopher, and the dread pedant Aristarchus, all seen in the late fourth *Dunciad,* are modern illustrations of Horatian decorum, vivid and vigorous in their specialties; but none seems to have been constructed on the basis of an inborn passion. Instead they are victims of foolish and socially ominous ideas, and any such masterful impulse in their make-up as pride is less important than their mistaken point of view. Probably by 1742, when the final book of the *Dunciad* was given to the foolish world, Pope had lost interest in the hypothesis.

Even in the early 1730's he wrote two striking sketches of characters for whom the "New Hypothesis" fails to supply an adequate explanation. Clodio (Wharton), says Pope, is a maze of extravagant and contradictory actions but can be understood as a man overmastered by a passion for praise.[5] But Pope puts too heavy a burden on one emotional tendency; eagerness for "gen'ral praise" does not quite open up this talented, witty, eloquent, refined man who could pray and whore, and mistreat wife, king, and friends. One senses an understructure of impulses quite as powerful as "the Lust of Praise." One might even suggest that the trouble with Wharton was that, driven by a restless mind and strong passions and, in addition, being blessed with talents, wealth, and great privilege, he unluckily had no *ruling* passion.

In the depiction of Marlborough[6] Pope mentions three "furies"—"Ambition, Av'rice and th' imperious Wife"—that govern this unheroic hero, and it is not made clear that any of these is a predominant passion. Although Pope told Spence that avarice was the key to the Duke's inconsistent behavior, in the verse-portrait that tendency has not "swallowed up" all the other passions. Possibly the choice of the word "furies" rather than "passions" for the three main forces in Marlborough's life indicates a half-conscious avoidance of the hypothesis so confidently explained in the second Book of a poem in which this sketch would appear in the fourth.

The farther one investigates Pope's use of the idea of a ruling passion, the less significant it appears to be. What could explain that

---

5. See above pp. 62-64, 67-68.
6. See above pp. 69-71.

strangest of charmers, Sylvia? The poet very sensibly does not say. What passion rules Sporus—malice? vanity? a craving for power? a love of evil? In the admirably lifelike picture of Atticus, which of the man's passions, vanity or envy or malice or, with all his advantages, timidity, is to be thought of as predominant? Criticism of Pope's art of drawing portraits is not much assisted by attention to the doctrine of the ruling passion. It was a notion that he found temporarily useful in his moral theory, but it fails to account for the timbre and power of many of his sketches. Simplicity was not what interested him in the world most, and neither ancient decorum nor the "New Hypothesis" could be the true basis of his view of Addison or Cloe or Bufo or Atossa or Cotta's droll son. If theory were needed to justify Pope's depicting such figures, it could have been found in certain other ideas then in the air—that is to say, in the books that were being read by Pope and his mentor Bolingbroke and by other people.

Later in the century Dr. Johnson was to observe of Shakespeare that in his day "Speculation had not yet attempted to analyse the mind, to trace the passions to their sources, to unfold the seminal principles of vice and virtue, or sound the depths of the heart for the motives of action."[7] But he could not have said that of Pope's day, which was beginning to feel the thrill, and profit from the study, of what in our entirely subjugated day is called psychology. Thomas Wright in *The Passions of the Minde* (1601), Cureau de la Chambre in *Les Charactères des Passions* (1640), Descartes in *Les Passions de l'Ame* (1649), Hobbes in *Leviathan,* and Walter Charleton, William Ayloffe, Isaac Watts, Francis Hutcheson, and David Hume, as the titles of works by each of them indicate, called this fascinating inquiry the study of the passions.[8]

---

7. Preface to *Shakespeare.*

8. Charleton's *Natural History of the Passions* appeared in 1674 but was advertised for sale as late as 1702 (in *The Adventures of Lindamira*). Ayloffe's *Government of the Passions* appeared in 1700 (second edition 1704), Watts's *Doctrine of the Passions* (second ed.) in 1732, Hutcheson's *Essay on the Nature and Conduct of the Passions and Affections* in 1728. Books IV and V of Nicolas Malebranche's *De la Recherche de la Vérité* (1674) considered the passions in a partly religious light as Ayloffe did. The second volume of Hume's *Treatise of Human Nature* (1739) was devoted to the passions, in, of course, a different spirit.

Aristotle and Aquinas had studied the passions too, as Johnson could have told us. But the attack on the subject made by Descartes and Hobbes was based upon very different notions of body and soul. Their work could be imagined to be in response to Bacon's plea for a study of the causes of difference in men's natures;[9] it undermined the simple old trust in recognizable types of men and disclosed beneath the surface a seeming chaos of passions, inclinations, instincts, and habits. To be sure, Descartes alluded to a few familiar categories—to generous people, to proud people, to the two kinds of men most likely to become victims of the two kinds of anger. But the generous and the proud are shown to be mixtures of passions, not permanent, separate types. Descartes would not have been interested in writing a Theophrastan Character of the Generous Man or the Proud Man or Pope's sketch of old Cotta or Helluo or vain Narcissa or the carnation-fancier. He cuts laterally through the types to get at the causes; he is a student of the elements within a man rather than of classes of men as elements in moral society.

So though Descartes especially pursued the six basic passions, he went on to chart their subdivisions and analyze their elaborate interactions and internecine wars. Dr. Charleton, physician to Charles II and a friend of Hobbes and Dryden, offered in his *Natural History of the Passions* a synthesis of ideas from Aristotle, Hobbes, Descartes, and others, not ignoring his own knowledge of medicine. He suggested a more intricate state of affairs than did his predecessors because he retained the notion, abandoned by Descartes, that there are two souls, the rational and the sensitive. Hutcheson's *Essay on the Nature and Conduct of the Passions and Affections* presents a still different analysis. Behind the passions we must recognize desires and aversions and "violent confused sensations." The automatic association of particular ideas with particular things and occasions further complicates the emotional life, as Descartes had more briefly indicated with the illustration of Marie de Medici's hatred of the fragrance of a rose.

---

9. *The Advancement of Learning*, Bk. II. See my *Theophrastan Character in England to 1642* (Cambridge, Mass., 1947), pp. 173-174.

As Bacon had foreseen, the desideratum of the seventeenth-century psychologist was to be the study of the differences between men, not their similarities. La Chambre in his Preface speaks of the "principal" or source of various aspects of a person; fearfulness produces avarice, dissembling, soft speaking, and so forth. Earlier than Descartes he opened up the infinitely complex spectacle of the inner life—major and minor passions, simple and mixed; motions of appetite and motions in action; spirits, humors, moral intentions; and all in a vast number of possible configurations.

Descartes, simplifying problems by discarding certain obsolete notions, implies that the peculiar nature of each man's brain is a primary cause; not a ruling passion but a controlling physique is the novelty he calls attention to. One stimulus may excite diverse passions in diverse men; it may render one man brave and another fearful. Pope's idea of the ruling passion is of a congenital force but less definitely physical than Descartes's conception of the basis of individual character. Hutcheson, somewhere between them, speaks of "Dispositions to some particular passions" but also of the old humoral " temperaments." The treatises as a group, even when retaining the religious attitudes of Augustine and Aquinas and opposing the heresies and impieties of the Cartesians, suggest to the reader the existence of an infinite number of categories of men rather than the traditional divisions mentioned by Aristotle and Horace, Theophrastus and Ben Jonson, Hall and Earle and Restoration drama.

So involved and mobile a structure of emotional busyness as the treatises disclose would naturally require much study on the part of anyone who would understand human nature. Hobbes's assertion[10] that the passions "are the same in all men" is prefatory to intricacy, not simple typicality. René Rapin, speaking of the problem of portraying characters in serious works of history, emphasizes the value of an understanding of the passions. He conceives of "essential and distinctive lines" for each person and of "singular and imperceptible Touches, by which alone Nature is express'd, and which are hardly found, otherwise than by a particular search into mens hearts, and a

---

10. *Leviathan*, Introduction.

discovery of all the Recesses thereof."[11] Isaac Watts in the Preface to his *Doctrine of the Passions* (second edition, 1732), in order to justify the preachment to follow, speaks of the innumerable and nameless "different Forms and Shapes in which our Passions appear, the sudden and secret Turns and Windings of them through the Heart, with the strange Mixtures and Complications of them in their continual Exercise." *Spectator* Number 408 solemnly declares that a study of the passions must precede any effort to comprehend how a man's action originates and proceeds.[12]

Everybody, it would seem, was learning about the passions. Even Richard Head's farrago of coney-catching and other materials, *Proteus Redivivus: or the Art of Wheedling* (1675), contained four chapters dealing with the passions and showing how the wheedler could prey upon them. Yet before the professional psychologists had commenced their labors and before the popular writers had begun to disseminate their teachings, Montaigne concluded his essay on the "Inconstancy of our Actions" with an apt warning: " '[T]is not all the understanding has to doe, simply to judge us by our outward Actions, it must penetrate the very Soul, and there discover by what springs the motion is guided: But that being a high and hazardous undertaking, I could wish that fewer would attempt it."[13] Pope, who declared to Spence that this essay was the "best in [Montaigne's] whole book,"[14] was duly impressed by the first part of this injunction.

The new psychology and the old law of decorum in characterization could of course be brought into some sort of harmony, and it is

---

11. *Instructions for History*, transl. J. Davis (1680), pp. 69, 79-80.

12. Shaftesbury in *Characteristicks* ("Advice to an Author," Part I, Sect. iii) said that a poet knows the "exact tones" and boundaries of the passions and makes use of this knowledge in his writing. Yet later in the same work (Part III, Sect. i) he ridiculed the pretensions and futilities of the professed students of the "inward resources of a human heart," particularly Descartes.

13. Cotton's translation (1686), which Bateson thinks Pope usually read (Bateson, p. 16 n.). Perhaps Pope listened also to the voice of his friend John Sheffield, Duke of Buckinghamshire, who remarked that since there are no two men exactly alike it was a pity that authors like Cicero and Bacon had not described the "implacableness of [men's] passions and humours" (Buckinghamshire's *Works*, ed. Pope [1723], II, 265— "On Authors").

14. Bateson, p. xxi.

appropriate that we should find in Dryden, who numbered Dr. Charleton among his friends, such a reconciliation. A poet, he declares, must understand the passions, "what they are in their own nature, and by what springs they are to be moved," so that each character will be shown to have a predominant passion and yet be different from all other characters.[15]

That a writer should hold in mind a controlling outline for the individual complexities of each of his dramatis personae was explained more elaborately by two subsequent authors. One was Mrs. Mary Delariviere Manley, whose knowledge of the passions was not altogether academic and yet who writes as if she had some acquaintance with the learned discussions. The writer of novels, she explains in the preface to *The Secret History of Queen Zarah* (1705), must have "Extraordinary Penetration" with which to distinguish the various combinations of the passions; "the Turn of the Mind, Motion of the Heart, Affection and Interests, alter the very Nature of the Passions, which are different in all Men." Yet in spite of these differences the novelist, in order "not to lose himself in this Labyrinth," should be sure to recognize the "predominant Quality, which ought to give the Spirit all the Motion and Action of our Lives."

The ancient theory of types and the new psychology met head-on in the long "Critical Essay on Characteristic-Writings" which Henry Gally printed as the introduction to his translation of *The Moral Characters of Theophrastus* (1725). Gally must have read Mrs. Manley or her sources; he is enthusiastically interested in the science of the passions, which every successful Character-writer must master. The "Heart of Man is frequently actuated by more Passions than one." Indeed a "Labyrinth of the Passions" fills the heart, and the writer must know the features of each emotion and its relation to the others. An "Affection of the Mind," exerting itself in different ways, lays a

Foundation for so many distinct Characters. The under Passions may, by their various Operations, cause some Diversity in the Colour and Complexion of the Whole, but 'tis the Master-Passion which must determine

---

15. Preface to *Troilus and Cressida*, "The Grounds of Criticism in Tragedy."

the Character . . . . A covetous Man may be impudent, or he may have some share of modesty left [like Pope's Marlborough, one might say]. On the other Hand, an Impudent Man may be generous, or his Character may be stain'd by Avarice. And therefore to make the features of one Virtue or Vice enter, as under Parts, into the Character of another Virtue or Vice, is so far from being a Transgression of the Nature of Things, that, on the contrary, all the Nicety of Characteristic-Writing, and all the Beauty which arises from the Variety of an agreeable Mixture, entirely depends on this. The main Difficulty consists in making the Master-Passion operate so conspicuously throughout the Whole, as that the Reader may, in every step of the Performance, immediately discover it.

Our souls are as different from one another "as our outward Faces are in their Lineaments." The writer of Characters must comprehend all these infinite differences; otherwise " 'twill be impossible ever to draw a Character so to the Life, as that it shall hit one Person, and him only."[16]

Thus Gally in his excitement has said that the imitator of Theophrastus, that great portrayer of familiar types, must draw portraits that fit only a single person! How Gally would, if challenged, worm his way out of this theoretical dilemma we need not pause to consider, though a guess might be formed on the basis of my introductory paragraphs in Chapter II. Gally's essay, available to Pope before he became interested in the "New Hypothesis," offers something of a parallel to certain of the pronouncements of Pope, who likewise accepted in the abstract the impressive notion of a "Master-Passion" and likewise felt the appeal of the picture that seems to "hit one Person, and him only."

It will be helpful to notice in sequence Pope's published discussions of his hypothesis. Spence's notes on the conversation about it in May, 1730, indicate that from the outset the idea of the ruling passion existed in Pope's mind in conjunction with a respectful attitude toward human inconsistency. In January, 1733, the *Epistle to Lord Bathurst* appeared, presenting briefly the idea that Heaven places a "ruling Passion" in men as a means of directing them toward ultimate good. Although Pope does not exactly say that in every person such

16. Pp. 31-35.

a passion exists, the reader may infer that it does. The theory is not elucidated, nor is it shown to be connected with the several bright sketches of type characters and of historical individuals that make up much of the poem.

Two months later, in Book II of the *Essay on Man*, Pope elaborated his theory, showing how the passions, though wild and unpredictable and

> born to fight,
> Yet mix'd and soften'd, in [God's] Work unite.

Pope devotes a good many lines to the subject, but in view of what the psychological treatises had been offering, the argument is not as explicit as it might be. One can see parallels in thought between what is said here and the doctrines of Aristotle and Aquinas, the old humors physiology, and the religio-moralistic psychology of Senault, Charleton, Malebranche, Ayloffe, and Hutcheson. Ayloffe's generously illustrated argument to show how God brings good out of "the disorderliness of Mans Passions" seems to be repeated by Pope.[17] Certain lines in the poem could remind one of Descartes:

> On diff'rent Senses diff'rent Objects strike:
> Hence diff'rent Passions more or less inflame,
> As strong, or weak, the Organs of the Frame.

But the central thought is not Cartesian. Of the six passions singled out by Pope to stand as the chief ones (ll. 107-108), only four—love, hate, joy, grief—have correspondence within the six that Descartes and his followers had so carefully considered.

Pope's discussion is neither systematic nor technical. Descartes had distinguished between passion, habit, and "inclination naturelle" (Sect. 171). Dr. Johnson, who was not unacquainted with the French philosopher's writings, complained that in the *Essay* Pope confounded

---

17. One of Ayloffe's sections is entitled "There is no Passion which may not be chang'd into a Virtue," and the idea is pervasive in his book. Maynard Mack's footnotes in his edition of the *Essay on Man* call attention to several close parallels with Ayloffe. See also my note in [Duke] *Library Notes*, No. 34 (Durham, N. C., 1959), p. 17.

passions, habits, and appetites. Somewhat elusive about fundamentals, Pope aimed not to chart the exact structure of the emotional system but rather to present a hopeful scheme by which men may be guided to better attitudes, better lives. His argument can be regarded also as a way of modernizing the ancient literary dogma of typicality and consistency in characterization; types are still to be thought of, but a good deal of activity of motive, volition, reason, and passion occurs beneath the surface of the category. As Mrs. Manley and Gally and the serious psychologists had shown, individual differences and even the workings of Providence affect what the superficial observer might regard as a type. But the all-powerful ruling passion as Pope conceived of it is special.

The *Essay on Man* offered no sketches to demonstrate the validity of its abstract principles. Ten months later, in the *Epistle to Lord Cobham,* Pope provided illustrations along with a new twist in his theorizing. Man's nature is full of "Quick Whirls" and "shifting Eddies," and each man differs from all others (l. 19). Tossed in a wild rotation of the passions, he frequently can understand neither himself nor his fellows. Plain characters we rarely find. The only part of a man that does not change is

> . . . in the ruling Passion: there, alone,
> The wild are constant, and the cunning known,
> The fool consistent, and the false sincere;
> Priests, Princes, Women, no Dissemblers here.
> This Clue once found unravels all the rest.

Then follows Pope's dazzlingly rhetorical sketch of the younger Wharton, chosen because of his being the most inconsistent of men. To explain so bizarre a figure Pope offers as a key the ruling passion of a lust of praise.

The sketch of Wharton and the new hypothesis are interesting to Pope, we now perceive, chiefly because of another theory here prominently developed—that man is almost universally inconsistent and unsteady. In the *Essay on Man* the latter doctrine hardly appeared. Yet Spence's note reveals that Montaigne's essay on man's perpetual inconstancy had impressed Pope, and indeed one can safely say that Montaigne helped shape the *Epistle to Lord Cobham*. Perhaps Horace, quoted by Montaigne, and Prior's essay on "Opinion" and Boileau's Satire VIII did too.[18]   One might be inclined to regard the idea of a ruling passion as now really minor if the *Epistle* were not rather surprisingly brought to an end in a striking series of sketches of plain types, consistent to their very last breaths. As far as doctrine is concerned, the total effect of the poem is equivocal. Pope was now moving toward another generalization about human nature that was to inform the *Epistle to a Lady*, issued a year later.

In the new poem, theorizing about human complexity is given a turn, as Mr. Bickerstaff would say, in honor of the ladies. "Most Women have no Characters at all," Pope pleasantly announces at the outset. In the beautifully contrived work that follows he presents sketch after sketch to uphold the truth of his opening remark. Changeable, contradictory, puzzling, yet ever charming, the ladies defy simple classification, but Pope imagines that one approximate division is possible:

> In sev'ral Men we sev'ral Passions find,
> In Women, two almost divide the Kind,
> Those only fix'd, they first or last obey;
> The Love of Pleasures, and the Love of Sway.

Four or five months later when Pope was revising the poem for inclusion in the octavo edition of his *Works* he dragged his "New Hypothesis" into the poem by substituting for the first of the four lines just quoted the line: "In Men we various Ruling Passions find." Thus we are made to suppose that women also are subject to a ruling passion. But the fact is that love of pleasure and love of sway are so vague and so inclusive that they help hardly at all in distinguishing one of these women from the next. When, in the set of his *Works* prepared for the Prince of Wales, Pope added to the poem the

---

18. "Ce qu'un jour il abhorre, en l'autre il le souhaite," says Boileau (VIII, 39); see also his tenth Satire. Bateson, p. 16 n., notices the probable sources in Montaigne and Prior.

sketches of Atossa and Philomede and, in the death-bed edition, the picture of Cloe he lessened the gaiety of the work and increased the difficulty of using the theory of the ruling passion to explain the characters of women.

Each of the main portraits in this gallery portrays a woman of such unexpected behavior that the reader is interested not in the simple governing passion (if it exists) but in the special inclinations, humors, passions, and habits that make each woman so peculiar. For depictions like these the Horation doctrine of types and the theory of a ruling passion are obsolete. The descriptive headings for the various sections of the poem added by Pope (or Richardson) in the footnotes in the octavo edition of the *Works* are likewise unsatisfactory: "Affected" is a poor label for Rufa; "Whimsical" fails to warn against the violence of Narcissa; "Witty and Refin'd" just begins to indicate Flavia's personality. Pope has now wholeheartedly adopted the idea, announced in the *Epistle to Lord Cobham,* that "each from other differs." He has seen beyond inconsistency to complexity. One is reminded, in Calypso and Narcissa and Atossa and Philomede and Cloe and Flavia, not so much of Montaigne's examples of unsteadiness as of the suggestions in the psychological treatises of the infinite variety and potential intricacy of men's motives, passions, and responses. Some of these women seem, in truth, cases more difficult than the writers of textbooks had envisaged.

Nor do I mean to propose that it was alone an acquaintance with the works on psychology and the passions that brought Pope to the point of view and the pictures of complexity displayed in the *Epistle to a Lady.* It would be foolish to imagine that someone as responsive to people as Pope was and as well established in sophisticated society needed to learn from books that men's characters are unsteady, involved, variegated. Nor is it possible to prove that he actually read any of the treatises, though evidence points fairly convincingly toward a knowledge of Ayloffe. The non-technical nature of his discussions of the passions indicates the adoption of no particular system of psychology and points to an affinity with Descartes's opponents. Pope's bookishness, if not also Bolingbroke's conversation, must have made him aware of what at least some of the authorities thought. Certainly Book Two of the *Essay on Man* shows that he was affected by the new psychology. But there is a work of a different, though related, sort which should be recognized as a possible influence on his doctrine of human inconsistency and on his enigmatic sketches, especially in the *Epistle to a Lady*. This is the *Caractères* of Jean de la Bruyère.

That La Bruyère and the author of the "Epistles to Several Persons" were in some respects kindred spirits is plain to anyone who reads their pages together. I have already remarked that as literary men familiar with the highest realms of society they picked similar kinds of people to describe. Pope expressed his admiration for the French writer in a letter to Judith Cowper in 1722: "The book you mention, Bruyere's Characters, will make any one know the world, & I believe at the same time despise it, (which is a sign it will make one know it thoroughly.) Tis certainly the proof of a Master-Hand, that can give such striking Likenesses in such slight Sketches, & in so few strokes on each subject."[19] Pope must have relished also the irony and the surprise that result from the seemingly casual application of the strokes. La Bruyère liked to reveal the nature of a person in hints and flashes or only at the end of a sketch in a key-sentence or by the one frank word in a piece of familiar wisdom. As has been noticed earlier, Pope also sometimes likes to reveal a character gradually. Technique exists for a purpose, and La Bruyère's purpose most of the time is to explore and expose the oddities in human nature, the self-deceptions and cross-purposes of the sophisticated, the blind spots in the eyes of writers and readers of books, the ambitions and failures and pomposities and lies of the habitués of the court, the sins of omission in a rigid society. Less disposed to preach than Pope, he draws a figure because it is interesting. Hence he portrays people who are credible but unfamiliar.

---

19. *Correspondence*, II, 142. Besides mentioning La Bruyère in another letter (II, 472-473), Pope quotes him three times: see the satiric "Advertisement" in the first edition of the *Dunciad* (1728); *Dunciad*, IV (1742), l. 524 n.; *Epilogue to the Satires Dialogue II*, l. 35 n. This last footnote, first printed in Warburton's edition of 1751 (IV, 321), was probably written in 1743 or 1744; see Butt, p. xxxix n.4.

Amidst the quietly devastating *pensées* and sketches that make up La Bruyère's chapter on women one comes upon a sentence that in idea and phrasing starts out like Pope's *Epistle to a Lady*. It is just one of the little drops of acid that placidly fall from La Bruyère's pen, eating away one's faith in life: "La plûpart des femmes n'ont gueres de principes, elles se conduisent par le coeur, dépendent pour leurs moeurs de ceux qu'elles aiment."[20] Pope keeps "plûpart," changes "scarcely" ("gueres") to "none at all," and drops the second part of the sentence as being untrue to a sex that is as changeable and unfixed as a cloud but also selfish, obstinate, and sometimes without affection: "Most Women have no Characters at all."[21] The same skepticism, now applied to the male sex, appears much later in La Bruyère's book and is given a paragraph of amplification: "Les hommes n'ont point de caracteres . . ."[22]——

Men have no certain Characters; or if they have any, 'tis that they have none which they always pursue, which never change, and by which they may be known. They are impatient in being always the same, in persevering either in Virtue or Vice. If they sometimes leave one Virtue for another, they are more often disgusted with one Vice for the sake of another. They have several contrary passions and weaknesses. Extreams are more easie to them, than regular and natural conduct, Enemies to moderation, excessive in all things, in good as well as evil, and when they cannot support, they ease themselves by changing.[23]

---

20. *Caractères*, I, 134.

21. There may be an echo in the poem of La Bruyère's idea presented two paragraphs earlier: it is astonishing, he says, that in some women the love of men is surpassed by ambition and play ("l'ambition & le jeu"). Pope, generalizing "jeu" and contradicting his own statement that women are too soft to bear a lasting mark, asserts that two passions "almost divide the kind"—"The Love of Pleasures, and the Love of Sway." La Bruyère regards the two passions that he mentions as fairly rare; Pope makes his pair the main ones.

Also Pope's lines beginning "Come then, the Colours and the ground prepare" may have been suggested by a later passage in La Bruyère: "Les couleurs sont préparées, & la toile est toute prête; mais comment le fixer, cet homme inquiet, leger, inconstant, qui change de mille & mille figures; je le peins devot, & je crois l'avoir attrapé, mais il m'echape, & déja il est libertin" (I, 414).

22. This parallel to the opening of Pope's *Epistle* (but not the former parallel) was noted in Elwin-Courthope (III, 95 n.).

23. *The Characters, or the Manners of the Age. By Monsieur De La Bruyère* (1700), p. 248.

Both the announced "truth" which the *Epistle to a Lady* develops and the related theory of almost ubiquitous human inconsistency which the *Epistle to Lord Cobham* proposes were foreshadowed by La Bruyère. The second of the two doctrines was one which La Bruyère, in seeming indifference to his apothegms about want of principles in women and of character in men, could utilize in the composing of character-sketches. In the chapter "Des Jugements" three figures are drawn whose essence is contradiction.[24] The first man, probably La Fontaine, appears gross and stupid but writes delicately, elegantly. The second man, probably Corneille, is timid, dull and stumbling in conversation, but invents heroes who speak like splendid kings and philosophers. The third, Théodas (probably Santeuil), is a sweet, easy, childlike man who suddenly thunders, rages, dazzles, and who possesses other prodigious contradictions. Théodas is not held together by anything in himself, but the description of him is held together rhetorically by the antitheses.

Strikingly expressive of La Bruyère's (and Pope's) doctrine is the sketch of "Un homme inégal [qui] n'est pas un seul homme, ce sont plusieurs":[25]

A Man unequal in his temper is several Men in one, he multiplies himself as often as he changes his Taste and Manners: He is not this Minute what he was the last, and will not be the next what he is now; he is his own Successor, ask not of what Complexion he is, but what are his Complexions; nor of what Humour, but how many sorts of Humours has he. Don't deceive yourself, is it Eutichrates whom you meet? How cold is he to Day? Yesterday he would have fought you, caress'd you and made his Friends jealous of you. Does he remember you? Tell him your Name.[26]

Wharton, we see, would have been a clearer illustration of the "homme inégal"—or the first lady in Pope's *Epistle:*

> How many Pictures of one Nymph we view,
> All how unlike each other, all how true!

---

24. *Caractères,* I, 375-376.
25. *Caractères,* I, 302.
26. *The Characters, or the Manners of the Age,* pp. 203-204.

There are other passages in the French book that keep the bewildering nature of men before the reader. An artist rather than a professional psychologist, La Bruyère does not supply technical analyses; but among his several hundred figures are many singular and opaque personalities, creatures talking in salons or passing through the court, with habits and manners mysterious enough to challenge the interest of the professionals. The ultimate in unfathomable human nature he obligingly presents at the end of his chapter on the court—Straton, a man to whom the stars have brought contradictory adventures and contradictory epithets, so that nothing has escaped his experience and he has baffled court opinion; a "caractere équivoque, mêlé, enveloppé: une énigme; une question presque indécise."

If Pope's Sylvia and Clodio-Wharton and Patritio and Calypso and Atossa and several others of his most interesting figures are not absolute enigmas, they none the less must have attracted Pope as they attract us because their natures are unresolved. Pope's mind was drawn to the complex personality. Such are Addison with his deviousness, Villiers with his mixture of wit and gaiety and social effectiveness and utter folly, and Marlborough to whom talent and ambition and love of money brought universal fame but who lacked the greatness of character to sustain it. To be sure, Pope also sketched traditional, simple types and pleases the reader with the vividness of the familiar; but the latter aesthetic effect is derived from something quite different from the peculiar privacies and exposed passions of Peter and Philomede and others who would equally have delighted La Bruyère. The poet's unchecked love of specific detail may explain the double nature of Fufidia and the multiple nature of the lawyer made from Donne's Coscus. Unchecked thrift may partially account for the mysterious characters of Calypso and Narcissa, two fragments of Sylvia. The inconsistencies in a few of Pope's people are in the mental point of view, not the character (Scoto and the "gay Freethinker" are of this sort), so that for them the question of a ruling passion is irrelevant. But in many of Pope's sketches a novel conjunction of under-passions seems the main source of power.

Comparison with Pope's recent predecessors will bring into clear light his tendency to build up a character of several components. Boileau, for example, had once said that if it were not too shocking he would describe a "Femme infernale" who is a settled atheist and trusts Destiny, not Heaven, as sovereign (*Sat.* X, 654-661). Pope not only dares to describe a woman (Flavia) who prays not to God but the stars, but he also shows several more elements in her nature that make her lamentable. William Law's conception of the self-indulgent, irreligious lady (also called Flavia) lacks the unexpected sense of decent behavior that complicates Pope's similar, cold-hearted Cloe.[27] Law's idle and shallow Caelia, harassed by no troubles except her own foolishness, is a simple case beside Pope's Flavia, whose discontentment comes partly from unusual intellectuality. Law's characterizations, lifelike though they usually are, serve as diagrams on which to erect sermons, and they necessarily portray plain, common dangers.

We should especially notice Edward Young's work in the seven satires published from 1725 to 1728 under the general title *Love of Fame the Universal Passion*. Pope could hardly avoid taking account of these galleries of pictures, though he was not an open imitator of Young as Young was of La Bruyère. Both Young and Pope (like Juvenal, Boileau, and La Bruyère) wrote "characteristical" satires on women, and one of the most important differences between their poems is in respect to complexity of character. Young drew Aspasia thus:

> Aspasia's highly born, and nicely bred,
> Of taste refin'd, in life and manners read,
> Yet reaps no fruit from her superior sense,
> But to be teaz'd by her own excellence.
> "Folks are so aukward! things so impolite!"
> She's elegantly pain'd from morn to night.
> Her delicacy's shock'd where-e'er she goes,
> Each creature's imperfections, are her woes.

---

27. See above, pp. 57-58.

> Heav'n by its favours has the fair distrest,
> And pour'd such blessings—that she can't be blest.[28]

Young's Syrena is not so much the impatient exquisite as the impatient intellectual:

> Syrena is for ever in extreams,
> And with a vengeance she commends, or blames.
> Conscious of her discernment, which is good,
> She strains too much to make it understood.
> Her judgment just, her sentence is too strong;
> Because she's right, she's ever in the wrong.[29]

Young's Tullia is a variant of Syrena:

> If Tullia had been blest with half her sense,
> None cou'd too much admire her excellence.
> But since she can make error shine so bright,
> She thinks it vulgar to defend the right.
> With understanding is she quite o'er-run;
> And by too great accomplishments undone.
> With skill she vibrates her eternal tongue,
> For ever most divinely in the wrong.[30]

Pope's Flavia, witty and voluble and exquisite and unrestrainedly intellectual and impatient, contains within herself Aspasia, Syrena, and Tullia, and is, besides, an avowed atheist and hedonist.[31]

Young portrays Lucia (Satire VI), who, loving the grandeur of wealth, "weds an Ideot; but she eats in plate." The woman in Pope's collection who "makes her hearty meal upon a Dunce" constitutes a less familiar case, for she (Philomede) is a drunken, lecherous peeress who is also a self-professed authority on fine taste in love. Young's Alicea is just a slattern, "the greatest Trapes in town." Pope's Arti-

---

28. *The Universal Passion. Satire VI. On Women* (1728), p. 9.
29. *Ibid.*, p. 11.
30. *Ibid.*, p. 6.
31. See above p. 52 for a male figure in Law's collection that has some resemblance to Flavia.

mesia is that, but she is also the mannish sort (Young's Thalestris [Satire V]) and the reader of Locke and Malebranche.

Pope's "great Atossa" has swallowed up the nature of Young's Cleora ("The height of avarice, and pride" [Satire VI]), of Syrena, and of Julia

> (Julia's a manager, she's born for rule,
> And knows her wiser husband is a fool [Satire VI]).

But it takes more than three of Young's women to constitute Atossa, a rare and amazing individual. Probably Pope began this picture with the awe-inspiring Duchess of Marlborough in mind[32] and then changed it in various details to represent more closely another fearful matron, the half-royal Duchess of Buckinghamshire.[33] Whoever Atossa was intended to be, the two ruling passions mentioned by Pope and the two kinds of anger discussed by Descartes rage in her, but the poet offers no simple key to her nature as he had mistakenly done for Clodio-Wharton. To say that she, like the other women in the poem, exemplifies consistent inconsistency is to mention only the shell; within is an intricate structure of volitions and passions, habits, and vices, physical traits and social temptations that makes her unique. To call her an individualized type would be to misrepresent the source of power in the picture. Of course Atossa may remind the reader of some actual woman he has had the dubious fortune of knowing; any portrait of an individual may cast glints of someone else, and Atossa has points in common, let us say, with Horace's Medea ("ferox invictaque"), the Lady Wishforts and Marwoods of Restoration comedy, and several of Young's matrons. But Pope's woman presents inner conflicts of special sorts and in an unusual degree; it is these *differentiae* as well as the ironic highlights that give the picture its depth and interest.

Philomede is another creation that includes not only inconsistency but also unexplained complexity. Joseph Warton's assertion that the lines about her were "designed for" Henrietta, the younger Duchess

32. Elwin-Courthope, III, 104 n.
33. Cf. Bateson, pp. 155-164.

of Marlborough, is one of those slightly belated eighteenth-century identifications that are now difficult to prove or disprove. Some details in the picture would seem to fit Henrietta; others as clearly would not.[34] The critic of Pope's art must take the piece for what in itself it offers.

> See Sin in State, majestically drunk,
> Proud as a Peeress, prouder as a Punk;
> Chaste to her Husband, frank to all beside,
> A teeming Mistress, but a barren Bride.
> What then? let Blood and Body bear the fault,
> Her Head's untouch'd, that noble Seat of Thought:
> Such this day's doctrine —— in another fit
> She sins with Poets thro' pure Love of Wit.
> What has not fir'd her bosom, or her brain?
> Cæsar and Tall-boy, Charles and Charlema'ne.
> As Helluo, late Dictator of the Feast,
> The Nose of Hau'gout, and the Tip of Taste,
> Critic'd your wine, and analyz'd your meat,
> Yet on plain Pudding deign'd at home to eat;
> So Philomedé, lect'ring all mankind
> On the soft Passion, and the Taste refin'd,
> Th' Address, the Delicacy —— stoops at once,
> And makes her hearty banquet —— on a Dunce.[35]

Among Pope's collection of women Philomede is the most outrageous. Haughty because a peeress, drunken, and more or less publicly lustful and promiscuous, she professes to be intellectual. Though arrogant in her debauchery (which includes lovers from all classes), she unaccountably likes to hold forth on refinement and delicate address and taste in love—and gladly accepts a dunce. Less charming than Sylvia, more abandoned than Atossa, and sillier than either, Philomede exceeds all expectation. She is, indeed, such an incon-

---

34. Cf. Bateson, pp. 54-55 n.

35. Quoted from what was apparently the earliest printing, the Prince of Wales's set of Pope's *Works*, II, "Ethic Epistles, The Second Book. To Several Persons," pp. 66-67, now in the Harvard University Library.

gruous mixture of characteristics that John Wilson Croker once proposed that Pope may have intended to depict one woman in the first
ten lines of the passage and another in the last eight, the former
woman "drunken, profligate, intriguing with all mankind from wits
to footmen, while Philomede may have done no worse than marry
a dunce."[36] Placed in the poem to climax a progression of three women
who oscillate between goodness and evil, she can be surpassed in
interest only by three women of greater gifts who follow her—Flavia
the passionate wit, Atossa the wisest fool which time has ever made,
and Cloe the beautifully decorous example of heartlessness. Atossa
and Flavia are all restless extravagance; but the behavior of Philomede, drawn in a slower tempo, exhibits unexpected quirks just as
Cloe's does and, for other instances among many, Sylvia's and Bufo's
and Marlborough's.

One might attempt to explain the oddities in Pope's characterizations by borrowing from Budgell his defense (and later Gally's) of
Theophrastus, who, he said, throws into a sketch a circumstance or two
which may not be illustrations of the nature of the class but serve "to
make the Picture of the Man Compleat." But this is not an adequate
reason for the complexities (except Cloe's) which I have mentioned.
Nor does Theophrastus really introduce contradictions of the main
feature of his type or details that diverge distractingly from what
one would suppose to be the main line. Neither is it helpful to consider Warburton's suggestion that women are driven by a desire to
hide their ruling passions (love of pleasure or of sway) into inevitable
inconsistency. Pope does not have that view of his women. The "New
Hypothesis" is in fact ignored in the *Epistle to a Lady* (and in the
Epistle to Dr. Arbuthnot, issued a month previously) because of a
greater interest in the antithetic elements in various remarkable
people, real and imaginary.

Pope's love of antithesis is well known. Yet some of his character-
sketches make almost no use of it. The two early pictures of the
happy retired man, the accounts of the blockhead critics, the dissi-

---

36. Elwin-Courthope, III, 101 n. That there is some attractiveness in Croker's
suggestion I have argued in Appendix B.

pated youth returning from the Grand Tour, the flower and butterfly fanciers, Villario, Aristarchus, the Man of Ross—all these exist
without contradictions in themselves and emerge in literary form
without benefit of antithesis. Not so Sylvia, with her bizarre charms,
nor Atticus, a conflict of appearance and reality, nor Sporus, that
"Amphibious Thing," nor Atossa, with all the advantages and none
of the satisfactions of life. In drawing Wharton Pope in unfortunate
imitation of Dryden's Zimri has produced a glittering series of
antitheses that unify the verse-paragraph and make it memorable but
not understandable. Pope's doctrine of man's almost universal inconsistency found an energetic verse-pattern that was less suitable for
the hypothesis of a ruling passion. Indeed Pope developed a habit of
progressing by oppositions and sometimes invented imaginary antitheses in order to give life to a creature not in himself very complex
or interesting. The first six lines of the epitaph on Lord Caryll which
he thriftily adapted for an epitaph on Sir William Trumbull[37] consist
entirely of antitheses, one of which ("An honest Courtier, and a Patriot too") Samuel Johnson complained of as being non-existent; "an
honest courtier cannot but be a patriot."

The problem in any description of personality of a complex sort
is to fuse the collected details into something that the imagination
can accept as a dynamic organism. The lawyer made from Donne's
Coscus, the Man of Ross, and Rufa are examples of Pope's somewhat
mechanical assemblage of traits and actions; the Man of Ross can
be easily understood, but the other two cannot. Many of the most
complex creations I have mentioned—Sylvia, Sporus, Flavia, Atossa,
for example—as well as such a simple type as the man presented in
the "Ode on Solitude" are unified by the poet's intensely emotional
perception.

Again a comparison with Young helps define Pope's accomplishment. Dr. Johnson regarded *Love of Fame the Universal Passion*
as "a very great performance" and had much to say about the justness
of its observations, its striking distichs and pointed sentences. He
complained, however, that although the figures were drawn with

---

37. Ault and Butt, pp. 81, 169-170.

nicety, Young "never penetrates the recesses of the mind." Johnson's complaint misses one aspect of the matter. Young does well enough with Lucia who loves to be rich, Julia the manager, Narcissus the idle society man (from La Bruyère), Flavia the vain, and many more. But these are a shallow lot. There are others, such as Syrena and Tullia, who are less familiar and somewhat less easy to understand. Yet because each is allowed to possess just one prominent feature, Young plunges at once to the secret of each with no suggestion of hidden difficulties or multiple causes. Hence his genuine wit and skilful versification are not enough to save the collection from monotony, especially since in size, method, and tone the sketches are generally uniform. Young sees about as much wrong with society as Pope does, but his evil and foolish figures are presented without complexity as his verse is without antithesis.[38] The world has seen many of Young's people before, and those it hasn't seen are plain enough not to be alarming. Not so Pope's less comprehensible folk in high life. Insisting on types and clinging fairly successfully to the one dominant passion of love of fame for all of his creations, Young is a better Character-writer, a truer Theophrastan, than Pope, but he is not a more interesting character-portrayer. For Pope notices the complications and unresolved tensions in human nature that Young usually ignores, and he consequently creates the impression of possessing greater depth and insight.

Like many another writer, Pope regarded people—his friends, his enemies, himself—as he regarded the forms and details of ancient and modern literature: all are proper material for modification. Perhaps the artist never sees anyone in life as merely what he is; the

---

38. It would be wrong to say that none of Young's figures are complex. But Philander (Satire III), though surprising in his behavior, seems to me a case either of unsuccessful analysis or of bad phrasing; Vincenna's variety of conduct (III), like that of La Bruyère's Ménalque, comes not from a complex nature but from incongruous and exaggerated illustration of the central trait; Phoebe (V), "proud of being rich in happiness" when she really is unhappy, must be a victim of something other than love of fame. Syrena, "for ever in extremes," is another woman whom Young sees as intricate but whose secret he has failed to discover. There are not many creatures in Young's poems as involved as these.

constant task is the shaping of designs. Pope wrote many kinds of character-sketches: subjective and objective, typical and individual, short and long, deep and superficial; characters revealed in dramatic dialogue and characters revealed by analysis; pictures of manners; outlines of a point of view; figures made vivid by a moment or a setting or a history; sketches moralized and sketches, a few of them, that merely amuse. In technique and subject-matter one can imagine indebtedness to the whole tradition, from Theophrastus down to Edward Young. But the merit which in Homer Pope praised above all else—invention, as Pope called it, or genius, to use Johnson's word for "a mind active, ambitious, and adventurous, always investigating, always aspiring"—this Pope had. He is original in presentation or in application if not in choice of subject. He may damage the universality of a type or create the *outré*, but he is constantly energetic. By the apt selection of a specific piece of behavior that expresses an essential trait and by the pungent employment of tangible images when the enlivening rhetoric of antithesis would be inappropriate he keeps his pictures fresh.

What stops the gallery-walker and holds him in delight and wonder may be a witty picture of a type, drawn to satisfy the classical taste, or it may be one of his remarkable portraits of complex and problematical people. Pope had at hand simple, oracular generalizations to justify both kinds of paintings; but the two contrary hypotheses of the ruling passion and of ubiquitous inconsistency, though they doubtless gave him help in the pursuit of human nature, probably do not alone account for his discoveries. It must have been his own cast of mind and feeling that drew him to tragi-comic spectacles of inadequacy and intensity among the fortunate, cases of frustration, examples of intellect, wealth, and high position leading to waste and unhappiness and defeat. Observation and intuition as much as reading made him sensitive to the subterranean and transverse impulses that cause some people to seem unique. In the sketching of these figures he departed from neo-classicism to inhabit the larger world of free and illimitable surprise.

APPENDIX A

POPE'S PORTRAIT of BETTERTON

THE portrait of Thomas Betterton reproduced as the frontispiece of the present volume by kind permission of the Earl of Mansfield appears to be a copy of Sir Godfrey Kneller's portrait of Betterton, now in the National Portrait Gallery. It has long been in the possession of the Earls of Mansfield. The first Earl, Pope's friend and one of his executors, once showed the picture to Sir John Hawkins, explaining that it was the only one Pope ever finished, "for that the weakness of his eyes was an obstruction to the use of the pencil" (Johnson's *Works* [1787], IV, 90, quoted in Johnson's *Lives of the English Poets*, ed. G. B. Hill [Oxford, 1905], III, 108 n.). Owen Ruffhead, presumably on the authority of Warburton, alluded to Pope's portrait of Betterton as being in the hands of Lord Mansfield (*Life of Alexander Pope* [1769], p. 477). The present Earl informs me that his father's grandfather, the fourth Earl, who was born only nine years after the death of the first Earl, spoke of the painting as by Pope.

William T. Whitley (*Artists and their Friends* [1928], I, 42-43) mentions with some suggestion of approval the assertion of a writer in 1785 that the painting was by Jervas rather than by Pope. It is of course quite possible that Pope had Jervas's help in the work. Norman Ault (*New Light on Pope*, pp. 73-75), running over the list of drawings and paintings thought to have been made by Pope, argues in defense of the attribution to Pope. One should notice in this connection that in the letter to Caryll (*Correspondence*, I, 189) in which Pope comically disparages his own painting he does say that his "masterpieces" have been a picture of Swift and one of Betterton.

The inventory of the furnishings of Pope's house at Twickenham (*Notes and Queries*, 6 ser., V [1882], 363-365) made at the time of his death includes "17 drawings by Mr Pope" kept in the "Garrets" and, among the large number of portraits hung about the house, all listed without mention of any artist's name, a "Pictture" of Betterton "in a Gold frame" in the "Chince Room fronting the Thames" and a "drawing" of Betterton "in a Black Frame" in the "Great Parlor."

Another figure-painting that is sometimes ascribed to Pope is the interesting variant of the engraved frontispiece of the 1745 edition of the *Essay on Man.* The frontispiece was designed by Pope but apparently, in spite of Warburton's assertion, not executed by him. Robert Carruthers in his *Life* of Pope (2d ed., 1857, pp. 90, 462-463) called attention to the painting. It presents a background that is very similar to that in the frontispiece of the 1745 volume, but the picture offers as its main feature a full-length figure of an extremely thin young man resting and leaning on the ruins. This figure has been regarded by some (see A. Edward Newton, *Pope, Poetry, and Portrait* [Berwyn, Penn., 1936]) as Pope's self-portrait, but the authentication of Pope's connection with the work is still not quite clear. The picture, now in the possession of Miss Caroline Newton, of Berwyn, Pennsylvania, is reproduced in Mack, opp. p. 11.

APPENDIX B

The "PHILOMEDE" LINES *in the* EPISTLE *to a* LADY

JOHN Wilson Croker's suggestion that the Philomede lines might have been intended to describe in turn two women is recorded in Elwin-Courthope, III, 101 n. These lines, as first printed, are quoted above, p. 126.

Croker thought that the two parts of the eighteen-line passage were "somewhat incongruous," as indeed they are. In the first ten lines "Sin in State" is a drunken, lustful, haughty peeress who pretends to intellectual interests which the poet mentions sarcastically ("that noble Seat of Thought"). To her inheritance from noble ancestors ("Blood and Body") she shifts the onus of her carnal behavior. Her passions or her mind have been "fir'd" by Caesar (some great man?), Tall-boy (the name of the sentimental young simpleton in Brome's old comedy *The Jovial Crew* and of an insatiable whore in Rochester's "The Argument"[1]), Charles (a footman?), and Charlemagne (some other great man?). Since none of these men sounds especially intellectual, one concludes that Pope again is implying the intensity and promiscuity of her sexual desires. If not a very familiar type, the debauched peeress is easily imaginable.

But by putting with these lines the remaining eight Pope complicates the whole in a way to make one wonder if there is something unresolved in the poetry as well as in the lady. If the drunken peeress is so lustful with wits, servants, and Caesar and yet seems as indifferent to public opinion as lines 2, 4, and 5 imply, why should she bother to lecture all mankind on refined taste and the soft passion and delicacy? Or even if this coarse and arrogant woman were inclined to profess delicacy, how could all mankind listen without laughing in her face? Or why, since she is so insatiable, is gobbling up a dunce particularly interesting? We have already heard of Tall-boy and Charles. Finally, even if she does amuse us by taking a dunce after lecturing everybody on delicacy in love, why should Pope bother to

1. I owe the former identification to Bateson, p. 55 n., and the latter to Stephen Blume.

say that she takes him heartily? What else would one expect of an un-inhibited "Punk" and teeming mistress? And, incidentally, there is not perfect aptness in the comparison of the profligate peeress with Helluo, whose fault is neither drunkenness nor lust.

If Croker's proposed division at "As Helluo" were made, the lines would present two clearly differentiated, though related, women—both inconsistent in their behavior, both pretending to be what they are not, both overruled by passion. But one is shocking and one merely absurd. The *Epistle to a Lady* is about female unsteadiness and inconsistency, and these would be two examples, developed in association as Rufa and Sappho are. The first ten lines would present an evil creature, a "noble" trafficker in sex, who shocks the satirist-poet; and the last lines would give us Philomede, an affected lady who like La Bruyère's inconsistent woman marries a dunce, thus amusing the humorist-poet.

Courthope rejected Croker's suggestion because he thought the place-ment of Pope's analytical headings argued against it. In the 1735 octavo *Works,* where these labels first appear, the heading for the lines describing Flavia is "Contrarieties in the Witty and Refin'd." In the death-bed edition the eighteen lines about "Sin in State" are inserted before the paragraph about Flavia with a new heading, "In the Lewd and Vicious." "Contra-rieties in the Witty and Refin'd" remains where it was, marking "Flavia's a Wit . . . ."

But the placement of the headings in the much-altered death-bed edi-tion may have been partly accidental, either the printer simply keeping the old headings where they were, or Pope or Warburton neglecting to indicate a necessary change. At least, if when the new lines were inserted the old heading ("Contrarieties in the Witty and Refin'd") had been moved back eight lines to include, with Flavia, the latter part of the new passage beginning at "As Helluo," all would have been as clear, though different: Helluo, with the "Tip of Taste" criticking your wine and then eating plain pudding at home, and Philomede, lecturing mankind on the "soft Passion, and the Taste refin'd" and then heartily accepting a dunce, are as cer-tainly as Flavia illustrations of contrariety in the refined and almost as plainly in the witty.

On the other hand, Warburton's footnote in the death-bed edition mentioning the newly inserted "Characters of Philomede, Atossa, Cloe" seems to indicate that he assumed that all eighteen lines dealt with Philo-mede. But Warburton was not always the subtlest or the fairest reader of Pope's verse, and because of the absence of indentation at "As Helluo . . ." (also conceivably due to someone's carelessness) he might easily have missed the point I am exploring. Professor Sherburn has called my attention to an absence of indentation in the text of the 1735 octavo *Works* just where one of the main divisions occurs ("Contrarieties in the Cunning and Artful").

So far as I am aware, all commentators except Croker have followed the implication of the printed paragraphing and have taken the entire passage as belonging to Philomede. But when Samuel Johnson in his *Life* of Pope remarked that what Pope said of Philomede was true of Prior, he must have been thinking only of the latter part of this verse-paragraph: the lecturer on the soft passion and on "The Address, the Delicacy" would be the neat poet and polite diplomat, and the dunce would be one of Prior's low-born mistresses, perhaps "Jinny the Just." Johnson could hardly have seen any connection between the bachelor poet and the striking image in the first ten lines of the passage.

If one prefers to think of Pope as likely to choose to portray types rather than complex individuals, Croker's suggestion should be appealing. But it is easier to float with the tide and take the traditional reading. For the present study, that reading is very acceptable.

INDEX